DATE			

THE PIANO WORKS OF SERGE PROKOFIEV

by
STEPHEN C.E. FIESS

The Scarecrow Press, Inc.
Metuchen, N.J., & London
1994

This work is based on the author's doctoral dissertation, "The Historical and Pedagogical Value of Prokofiev's Published Music for Solo Piano." Boulder: University of Colorado, 1989.

Frontispiece: Serge Prokofiev. From James Camner (ed.), *Great Composers in Historic Photographs.* New York: Dover, 1981.

British Library Cataloguing-in-Publication data available

Library of Congress Cataloging-in-Publication Data

Fiess, Stephen C. E., 1956-
    The piano works of Serge Prokofiev / by Stephen C. E. Fiess
        p.   cm.
    Based on the author's doctoral dissertation from the University
of Colorado, Boulder.
        Discography: p.
        Includes bibliographical references and index.
        ISBN 0-8108-2901-0 (acid-free paper)
        1. Prokofiev, Sergey, 1891-1953--Piano music.   2. Piano
music--Analysis, appreciation.   I. Title.
MT145.P8F54   1994
786.2 ' 092--dc20   94 -13606

To my parents,
the late Rev. Philip Fiess II
and Mrs. Grace Nicholson Fiess,
and to my first piano teacher,
Mrs. Josephine Parrott,
who started me on my life-long journey
into the world of music

ACKNOWLEDGMENTS

I would like to acknowledge the many individuals who assisted in various ways in the preparation of this book. First of all, I want to thank Mr. Neal Wegener, without whose assistance this book would not have been published, for his countless hours spent in word processing, proofreading, editing, and manifold other tasks related to the production of both the manuscript and the finished copy of this book. I would next like to thank Mr. Kevin Kennedy, Chairman of the Music Department at Arapahoe Community College, Littleton, Colorado, for his tireless efforts in transcribing, proofreading, and printing the computer-engraved musical examples for this book.

I would like also to thank concert pianist Barbara Nissman, eminent Prokofiev interpreter and recording artist, for her insightful foreword and advice; Professor James Bratton, professor emeritus of organ and theory at the University of Denver, for providing valuable information regarding Prokofiev's piano rolls; and Mr. Donald Hilsberg, for his excellent proofreading and editorial advice. I would also like to acknowledge the following individuals who have contributed important information and research time pertaining to various portions of the text and discography: Professor Rob Hallquist of the University of Northern Colorado at Greeley; Mr. Mark Carpenter, Mrs. Sheila McKay, Mr. Rodney Mobley, Mrs. Kristine Palumbo, and Ms. June Tomastick.

I would also like to thank G. Schirmer, Inc. and Boosey & Hawkes, Inc. for granting permission to use the musical examples from Prokofiev's piano works. I would also like to thank my professors of piano and piano literature, especially Dr. Damiana Bratuz of the University of Western Ontario, Canada. Last, but not least, a very special thanks to my family and friends for their encouragement and support.

CONTENTS

v

FOREWORD

Francis Poulenc called him the "Russian Liszt," and certainly no other composer of the twentieth century has demonstrated such natural pianism and keyboard virtuosity, nor produced such a substantial piano repertoire. Serge Prokofiev can indeed be considered the heir apparent to Franz Liszt, for he carried the Romantic tradition of pianism into the twentieth century and exploited it beyond its known limits.

Endowed with natural facility as a pianist, Prokofiev could intuitively build upon the foundations of Romantic pianism, concentrating on sonority and virtuosity, while forging his own idiom at the keyboard. Exploiting the inherent rhythmic energy of the toccata and motoric patterns, Prokofiev created his own brand of virtuosic excitement. He also extended the concept of melody and line inherent in Romantic piano music and directed it into a personal lyricism that is evident in even his most virtuosic writing and is also essential to an understanding of his work.

Prokofiev built upon the tonal harmonic tradition of the nineteenth century and expanded it into his twentieth-century language, creating in the process his own brand of dissonance. A preoccupation with form and structure is apparent in all his works, to which he brought great sophistication and the ability to mold the structure to accommodate the musical line. He was able to shape a work profoundly within the limits of his formal framework, using the same skills that, incidentally, made him a superb chess player. His links to Beethoven are evident in his adherence to sonata form, compositional techniques of motivic transformation, and economy of material. And the Romantic voice of Robert Schumann echoes clearly in Prokofiev's character pieces.

Prokofiev seemed most comfortable and most adventurous when writing for the solo piano. His affinity for the keyboard was nurtured from infancy by his mother, herself an amateur pianist, and he developed his pianistic talents at the St. Petersburg Conservatory to a level that later enabled him to earn his living for fifteen years primarily as a touring pianist. It was this knowledge of the keyboard that allowed Prokofiev to write music that, no matter how technically demanding, always fits well under the fingers—it is always pianistic and always a joy to perform.

Nevertheless, the question must be asked as to why Prokofiev's solo piano music, outside of a few "warhorses," has generally been neglected both in the concert halls and in the teaching repertory. For some, he is too conservative, too old-fashioned, a hold-over from the nineteenth century; for others, he is too "modern," too percussive and brittle, and too unemotional. Clearly our century has not yet come to terms with Prokofiev's place within its musical history.

The more I study the music of Prokofiev, the more I realize the extraordinary scope of his twentieth-century contribution to the pianistic tradition. The solo repertoire of Bartók and Stravinsky did not develop in this direction. Indeed, this century has not produced any composer whose contribution to the solo piano literature can approach that of Prokofiev. As Bartók's achievement is now perceived as a great modernist meditation upon tradition, and Picasso understood so well that "without tradition, there can be no art," so stands the solo piano music of Prokofiev. I believe that the next century shall perceive this solo literature as one of the monumental achievements of twentieth-century art. That this achievement was not appreciated in its own day is, in itself, within a great tradition.

Barbara Nissman
Lewisburg, West Virginia

INTRODUCTION

Serge Prokofiev (1891-1953) may rightly be regarded as one of the most prolific and successful composers of serious piano music in the twentieth century. A catalogue of his piano works includes nine sonatas (plus an unfinished tenth and eleventh), four etudes, three sonatinas, one toccata, seventy-two shorter pieces for piano, and forty-six transcriptions based upon orchestral works and excerpts from his opera, ballet, and film scores. While such a catalogue immediately impresses by its length alone, it is nevertheless safe to say that Prokofiev's reputation as one of the great masters of twentieth-century piano literature rests less upon his productivity than upon the originality, individuality, and craftsmanship of his piano compositions.

The recent celebration of the centennial of Prokofiev's birth makes this a particularly appropriate time to discuss the continuing historical and pedagogical importance of Prokofiev's music for solo piano. This book will first focus upon the aesthetics and historical context of Prokofiev's piano music, and will then provide a pedagogical introduction to his piano works for soloist, teacher, and student.

Chapter One will examine the aesthetics of Prokofiev's piano music. Contemporary musical and aesthetic trends will be discussed, along with Prokofiev's personal reactions to these trends.

Chapter Two will supply a brief historical background describing Prokofiev's career as a composer. It will also examine stylistic characteristics of Prokofiev's piano works in relation to innovations in style in the piano music of his contemporaries. Specifically, the piano music of Prokofiev will be discussed as the product of three major periods in his life: the Russian period, the foreign period, and the Soviet period. His treatment of harmony, melody, rhythm, texture, form, and pianistic technique will be examined in light of contemporary trends and Prokofiev's own changing aesthetic goals.

In the third chapter, Prokofiev's piano music will be divided into four categories: pedagogical works, advanced-intermediate-level works, advanced-level or concert works, and transcriptions. Each work will be examined briefly for its pedagogical and artistic merits or, in some cases, its perceived deficiencies.

In the final chapter, an attempt will be made to draw some brief conclusions regarding Prokofiev's position as a composer for the piano.

Chapter I

THE AESTHETICS OF PROKOFIEV'S PIANO MUSIC

Prokofiev once stated that he wanted to create "an entirely new music."[1] In many ways, his music does succeed in being different from any music that came before it. Even so, Prokofiev was not the type of musical revolutionary who wished to dispense totally with tradition for the purpose of creating music that was entirely original. Prokofiev himself acknowledged his indebtedness to tradition. Throughout his career, he retained a deep respect for many of the great composers of the Western European musical tradition, and he often drew upon the forms and techniques of past masters, without fear of sacrificing his own individuality.

Of the Viennese Classicists, Prokofiev admired Beethoven more than Mozart or Haydn, despite the allusions to the music of Mozart and Haydn in Prokofiev's *"Classical" Symphony*, Opus 21. The influence of Beethoven is felt in Prokofiev's scherzo movements, in his perpetual motion movements, and in what Leonid Sabanieff has called a "Spartan spirit."[2]

Some writers have pointed out the influence of other composers upon Prokofiev's piano compositions. The rapid leaps, hand-crossings, and glissandi recall Domenico Scarlatti. The Romantic writing of the first piano *Sonata* is reminiscent of Schumann, Brahms, and Rachmaninoff. Certain modernized Alberti-bass patterns recall Mozart and Haydn.

Sometimes, particular pieces served as models or sources of inspiration for Prokofiev. For instance, Prokofiev once cited Saint-Saëns's arrangement of a Bach gavotte as a source of inspiration for Prokofiev's own gavottes.[3] Prokofiev's admiration for Schumann's *Toccata*, Opus 7, was a key factor contributing to the dominant role of the toccata or motoric element in Prokofiev's piano writing.[4]

1

Prokofiev's music derives much of its strength and accessibility from associations with previous musical styles, associations that often serve to highlight his stylistic innovations. A number of Prokofiev's works have been labelled neo-Classical because of their synthesis of Classical clarity of form and contemporary compositional techniques. Other compositions of Prokofiev have been labelled neo-Romantic because of their synthesis of Romantic aesthetics and contemporary harmonies. In many of his works, neo-Classical passages and neo-Romantic passages exist side-by-side.

Prokofiev was a prominent figure among those composers who experimented with neo-Classical aesthetics. Neo-Classicism, as an artistic movement, rebelled against the aesthetics of nineteenth-century Romanticism by returning to ideals, forms, and techniques of more distant musical periods, particularly the Classical and Baroque periods. Following the lead of composers such as Erik Satie [*Trois sarabandes*, 1887], Claude Debussy ["Sarabande" from *Suite Pour le piano*, 1901], and Maurice Ravel ["Menuet" from *Sonatine*, 1905], Prokofiev carried on the revival and modernization of Baroque and Renaissance dances in several gavottes, rigaudons, allemandes, and other pieces based upon dance styles.

Prokofiev's second piano *Sonata*, Opus 14 (1912), is one of the landmark works of neo-Classicism. The simplicity of many of its textures, the symmetry and tightness of phrasing and structure, combined with the novel harmonies and melodies, and touches of ironic humor make this work one of Prokofiev's most original achievements. As David Kinsey observes, this work paved the way for such later neo-Classical works as Stravinsky's piano *Sonata* (1924).[5]

As already noted, Prokofiev was not solely a neo-Classicist. Many of Prokofiev's works also show the influence of neo-Romanticism, a movement that retained the aesthetics of nineteenth-century Romanticism while infusing new life through the use of contemporary harmonic and melodic techniques. The lush melodies of the slow movements of the sixth, seventh, and eighth *Sonatas* (Opp. 82, 83, and 84) attest to the fact that Prokofiev never totally rebelled against Romanticism, despite the strong currents of anti-Romantic sentiment in the twentieth century. As a lyricist, Prokofiev wrote music that was sometimes sentimental, sometimes deeply Romantic in feeling. As David Kinsey notes, Prokofiev's Romanticism is often evidenced by his marks of expression, for example, "caloroso," "tenebroso," "inquieto," "tranquillo," and "con agitazione e dolore."[6]

Prokofiev's piano pieces show the influence of several twentieth-century trends in music and the arts, and the rejection of others. In addition to neo-Classicism and neo-Romanticism, the aesthetic trends that were strong during Prokofiev's lifetime include impressionism, expressionism, surrealism, mysticism, primitivism, futurism, folklorism, and "socialist realism."[7] Prokofiev disdained impressionist or symbolist aesthetics as practiced by Debussy and Ravel. Prokofiev acknowledged the technical mastery of these two composers, particularly Ravel, although he did not share, to the same degree, their enthusiasm for impressionist aesthetics. On one occasion, Prokofiev referred to Debussy's music as "jelly...absolutely spineless music...except perhaps, it's very 'personal' jelly and the jellymaker knows what he's doing."[8]

Prokofiev also remained largely untouched by Surrealist and mystical aesthetics. The mysticism of composers such as Alexander Scriabin and Erik Satie was essentially foreign to Prokofiev's personal nature, despite the Scriabinesque mysticism evident in some of Prokofiev's earlier works, including several of the *Visions fugitives,* Opus 22 (1915-1917). Prokofiev's early infatuation with Scriabin's music is shown more in the influence of Scriabin's harmonic practice upon Prokofiev's stylistic development, than in Prokofiev's aesthetics. For the most part, Prokofiev preferred a musical aesthetic that was down-to-earth and robust rather than mystical or ethereal.

The *Toccata,* Opus 11 (1912), and the finale of the seventh *Sonata,* Opus 83 (1939-1942), represent one extreme of Prokofiev's range of aesthetics. In these particular works, Prokofiev embraced expressionist, primitivist, and mechanistic aesthetics.

Expressionist aesthetics in the visual arts tend to revel in depicting anxiety (Edvard Munch, *The Scream,* 1893) and an accordingly distorted or nightmarish view of reality (James Ensor, *Masks and Death,* 1897). Expressionistic music tends to embrace extreme dissonance and rhythmic drive. Prokofiev's *Toccata,* Opus 11 (1912), probably has the most consistently relentless rhythmic drive of any piece written up until its time. It was not the first expressionistic piece for piano, however. Schoenberg's "Klavierstück," Opus 11 #3 (1908), was written four years before the Prokofiev *Toccata.* Bartók's *Allegro barbaro* (1911) also predates the Prokofiev *Toccata.*

Abstract expressionism in the visual arts, exemplified by the work of Wassily Kandinsky, involves the total discarding of concrete subject matter in favor of abstract shapes, colors, and lines. An analogous development in music is Schoenberg's rejection of tonality and thematicism in favor of athematic, atonal music that exemplifies his principle of "emancipation of the dissonance."[9]   Although Prokofiev sometimes embraced expressionism, he rejected abstract expressionism; even his most expressionistic piano works retain, at most times, a clear sense of tonality, together with clarity of phrasing and structure.

Primitivism as a twentieth-century movement in the arts owes much to the exploration of primitive cultures.   For example, Picasso's *Les Desmoiselles d'Avignon* (1907), which was a landmark of Cubist primitivism, includes a female figure that has a stylized African mask for a face.   Primitivism in music relies upon elements of primitive music—particularly repetition of short motives that have a small range of pitch.   Prokofiev's "Diabolical Suggestion," Opus 4 #4 (1908, revised in 1911), could be said to be the first primitivist piano piece or at least the first to foreshadow full-fledged primitivism as exemplified by Bartók's *Allegro barbaro* (1911) and Prokofiev's *Toccata* (1912). We should bear in mind that all of these works predate Stravinsky's primitivist ballet, *The Rite of Spring* (1913).

The *stile mécanique*[10] (mechanistic style) is exemplified by several early works of Prokofiev.   Repeated figures that suggest imaginative associations with the movement of pistons, clockwork mechanisms, and other mechanical actions appear in certain piano works by Prokofiev, for example, *Toccata*, Opus 11; *Sonata #2, Opus 14*; and *Sonata #7, Opus 83*.

Prokofiev was not the first artist to adopt a mechanistic aesthetic.   The first major artistic movement to focus upon the machine in painting, sculpture, and music was the Italian Futurist movement;[11] in 1913, Luigi Russolo, one of the leaders of this movement, gave a concert of Futurist noise-music.   However, while Russolo was experimenting with "noise instruments," Prokofiev was adapting machine aesthetics to piano music in his *Toccata* (1912) and in several sections of his second piano *Sonata* (first movement, transition; scherzo, opening theme; and finale, accompaniment to the second subject).

Folklorism, another strong current in twentieth-century music, is much less evident in Prokofiev's music than in the music of two of his contemporaries, Béla Bartók and Zoltán Kodály, both of whom engaged in extensive ethnomusicological field-work.   The creation of folkloristic Russian music was not one of Prokofiev's major goals, although during his Soviet period, he did collect folk tunes for his second *String Quartet* ("Kabardinian"), Opus 92 (1941); his opera *The Story of a Real Man,* Opus 117 (1947-1948); and his ballet *The Stone Flower,* Opus 118 (1948-1953).

After Prokofiev's return to his native land in 1936, he wrote more works based upon Russian subjects, partly because of his love for Russia, and partly because of political pressures. Under the Communist regimes of the Union of Soviet Socialist Republics, composers were expected to adhere to an aesthetic of "socialist realism," and to create works that would inspire the masses through simplicity, optimism, nationalism, and glorification of life in the Communist state. Composers who did not comply were accused of succumbing to Western "formalism," which included all the "dangerously decadent" trends in twentieth-century Western art towards abstraction, pessimism, and dissonance.

Although Prokofiev's own musical aesthetic tended naturally towards simplicity and optimism, thereby coinciding to an extent with official Soviet artistic dictates, his relations with the Soviet government were often uneasy. Ironically, those works that gained the most official favor were usually his most abstract ones, for example, the sixth, seventh, and eighth *Sonatas*—all works that received Stalin prizes. His attempts to curry favor with the Soviet leadership through the use of texts on political themes [for example, *Cantata for the Twentieth Anniversary of the October Revolution,* Opus 74 (1936-1937)] often met with less success.

A discussion of Prokofiev's aesthetics would not be complete without mention of his sense of humor. Prokofiev frequently delighted in musical irony: parodies of dances and marches, unexpected twists in melody and harmony, grotesque use of the low register of the piano, and ridiculous insistence upon incongruous elements.

Sometimes, in Prokofiev's work, the *stile mécanique* acquires an ironic tone, as if to parody the machine age. Prokofiev's occasional parodies of the machine age could be said to foreshadow such later masterpieces of art and film as Paul Klee's painting *Twittering Machine* (1922), and Charles Chaplin's film *Modern Times* (1935).

Part of the enduring popularity of Prokofiev's music lies in his successful synthesis of diverse techniques and aesthetically wide-ranging, yet appealing, musical ideals: classicism, Romantic lyricism, expressionism, and ironic humor. Prokofiev once referred to his five lines of musical development as being "the classical line," "the modern trend," "the toccata or 'motor' line," "the lyrical line," and "the 'scherzoish' line."[12]   In discussing Prokofiev's successful synthesis of technique and aesthetics, author David Kinsey notes:

> He [Prokofiev] achieved more nearly than some of his contemporaries a balance between intellect and emotion, between content and technique, between spontaneity and constructivism.   If he sometimes failed to weave the separate strands into a single cohesive fabric, these exceptions merely highlight the fact that he succeeded more often than he failed.[13]

Another important factor contributing to Prokofiev's popularity as a composer may well be his rather forthright attitude to musical composition.   Unlike some contemporary musicians such as Schoenberg or Hindemith, Prokofiev did not attempt to codify a theoretical system based upon his own innovations, nor did he base his musical practice upon pre-conceived theoretical ideas.   He once stated, "I have no theories.   I am essentially a pupil of my own musical ideas."[14]   Perhaps one particular explanation of Prokofiev's method of composition ought to be acknowledged, yet taken with a grain of salt: when questioned about his father's method of composition, Prokofiev's eldest son, Sviatoslav, once replied, "My father writes music like other people's and then Prokofievizes it."[15]

Chapter II

PROKOFIEV'S PIANO MUSIC IN HISTORICAL CONTEXT

Prokofiev's aesthetic principles soon found their musical realization in the form of stylistic innovations and the creation of what may be considered his personal style. Although each of Prokofiev's works is unique, Prokofiev adhered fairly consistently throughout his life to techniques established in his early works. His style did not remain static, however, since his aesthetic principles continued to evolve and mature, and he continued to experiment with new techniques and to build upon established ones.

Historians usually divide Prokofiev's life and work into three periods: the Russian period (1891-1917), the foreign period (1918-1935), and the Soviet period (1936-1953). Following that plan, this chapter will discuss Prokofiev's treatment of harmony, melody, rhythm, texture, form, and pianistic technique in those piano works that date from each of these periods. This chapter will also attempt to place Prokofiev's piano works in historical context by examining them in relation to trends and techniques in selected piano works of his major contemporaries.

The Russian Period (1891-1917)

Biographical Notes

Serge Prokofiev was born on April 23, 1891, in the village of Sontsovka in the Ukraine. With the help and guidance of his mother, an accomplished amateur pianist, he wrote his first piano pieces at the age of five.

7

In 1902, Prokofiev's mother persuaded the composer Reinhold Glière to spend the summer at Sontsovka tutoring her eleven-year-old *Wunderkind* who had already composed two operas and several piano pieces. Glière spent many hours during the summers of 1902-1904 teaching Prokofiev the disciplines of harmony, form, and orchestration.

In 1904, the composer Alexander Glazounov persuaded Prokofiev's parents to allow their son to enter the St. Petersburg Conservatory. During his ten years at the conservatory, Prokofiev studied harmony and counterpoint with Anatole Liadov, orchestration with Nicholas Rimsky-Korsakov, conducting with Nicholas Tcherepnin, and piano with Alexander Winkler and Annette Essipova. He also became friends with Boris Asafyev and Nicholas Miaskovsky. During his conservatory years, Prokofiev's interest in contemporary music was given impetus by the composer Max Reger's visit to St. Petersburg in 1906, and by the St. Petersburg premiere of Scriabin's *Poem of Ecstasy* in 1907.

While a student at the conservatory, Prokofiev also began to attend a series of concerts in St. Petersburg known as the Evenings of Modern Music. He was invited to make his debut there as pianist-composer in 1908.

In 1911, Prokofiev had some of his early piano pieces published. In that year, he also gave the debut of his first piano *Concerto* and introduced the piano music of Schoenberg to Russia. The second piano *Concerto* and the *Toccata* followed a year later.

In 1914, Prokofiev visited London, where he met Stravinsky and Diaghilev and saw Stravinsky's *Nightingale, Firebird, Petrushka,* and *The Rite of Spring,* as well as Ravel's *Daphnis and Chloë.* Prokofiev soon began work on two ballets for Diaghilev: *Ala and Lolli* and *Chout* (or *The Buffoon*). Before leaving Russia in the aftermath of the 1917 revolution, he also completed several works, including an opera on Dostoyevsky's *The Gambler,* the first *Violin Concerto,* the *"Classical"* Symphony, and the third and fourth piano *Sonatas.*

Style in Prokofiev's Russian-period Piano Works

Before proceeding with a stylistic discussion of Prokofiev's Russian-period piano works, it is helpful to know the title and date of composition of each of these works. As the following list shows, some of Prokofiev's early piano works were published in an order different from the chronological order of their composition. Also, some of these works were revised greatly before publication. The following list includes all of Prokofiev's piano works that were published during his Russian period and gives, in most cases, the dates of their actual composition:

Opus 1,   *Sonata #1*, F minor, 1909 (after an unpublished *Sonata*, 1907)
Opus 2,   *Four Etudes*, 1909
Opus 3,   *Four Pieces*, 1911 (revision of *Four Pieces*, 1907-1908): "Story," "Jest" or "Badinage," "March," "Phantom"
Opus 4,   *Four Pieces*, 1908-1912 (revision of *Four Pieces*, 1908): "Reminiscences," "Elan," "Despair," "Diabolical Suggestion"
Opus 11, *Toccata*, D minor, 1912
Opus 12, *Ten Pieces*, 1906-1913: "March," "Gavotte," "Rigaudon," "Mazurka," "Capriccio," "Legend," "Prelude," "Allemande," "Humoresque Scherzo," "Scherzo"
Opus 14, *Sonata*, D minor, 1912
Opus 17, *Sarcasms*, 5 pieces, 1912-1914
Opus 22, *Visions fugitives*, 20 pieces, 1915-1917
Opus 28, *Sonata #3* (from old notebooks), A minor, 1917
Opus 29, *Sonata #4* (from old notebooks), C minor, 1917 (after *Sonata #5*, 1908 and *Symphony*, 1908)

By the time of the publication of the *Sonata*, Opus 1, the young Prokofiev had already composed many other piano works that still remain unpublished, including several collections of short piano pieces, which he called "Little Songs" or "Ditties." However, a comprehensive discussion of the unpublished works is beyond the scope of this book.

In assessing the historical importance of Prokofiev's early piano works, it is helpful also at this point to list the most significant piano works written during the same period or shortly before by Prokofiev's major contemporaries. It then becomes possible to point out historical links between many of these works and the early piano works of Prokofiev. Works selected from the following list will serve to illustrate developments in piano music that are roughly contemporary with the creation of Prokofiev's Russian-period piano works:

Works by composers in France:

Debussy:

1903:	*Estampes*
1904:	*L'isle joyeuse*
1905:	*Images,* Book I
1906-08:	*Children's Corner*
1907:	*Images,* Book II
1909:	*The Little Negro*
1910:	*Préludes,* Book I
1912-13:	*Préludes,* Book II
1915:	*Etudes*

Ravel:

1901:	*Jeux d'eau*
1903-05:	*Sonatine*
1904-05:	*Miroirs*
1908:	*Gaspard de la nuit*
1911:	*Valses nobles et sentimentales*
1914-17:	*Le tombeau de Couperin*

Satie:

1887:	*Trois sarabandes*
1888:	*Trois gymnopédies*
1888:	*Trois gnossiennes*
1893:	*Vexations*
1914:	*Sports et divertissements*

Works by composers in Russia:

Scriabin:

1907:	*Sonata #5; Désir*
1907:	*Caresse dansée*
1911:	*Sonata #6,* Opus 62
1911:	*Deux poèmes*
1911:	*Sonata #7,* Opus 64 *("White Mass")*
1912:	*Trois études,* Opus 65
1912-13:	*Sonata #8,* Opus 66
1912-13:	*Deux préludes*
1912-13:	*Sonata #9,* Opus 68
1912-13:	*Sonata #10,* Opus 70
1912-13:	*Deux poèmes,* Opus 69
1914:	*Vers la flamme*
1914:	*Deux danses*
1914:	*Cinq préludes*

Stravinsky:

1908:	*Four Etudes,* Opus 7

Rachmaninoff:

1911:	*Etudes-tableaux,* Opus 33
1913/31:	*Sonata #2,* Opus 36
1916-17:	*Etudes-tableaux,* Opus 39

Works by composers in Vienna:

Schoenberg:

1909:	*Drei Klavierstücke,* Opus 11
1911:	*Sechs Kleine Klavierstücke,* Opus 19

Berg:

1908:   *Sonata,* Opus 1

Works by composers in Hungary:

Bartók:

1904:	*Rhapsody,* Opus 1
1908:	*Fourteen Bagatelles,* Opus 6
1908-09:	*Two Dirges,* Opus 8B
1908-09:	*For Children*
1909-10:	*Two Roumanian Dances,* Opus 8A
1908-10:	*Seven Sketches,* Opus 9B
1908-11:	*Three Burlesques,* Opus 8C
1909-10:	*Four Dirges,* Opus 9A
1911:	*Allegro barbaro*
1916:	*Suite,* Opus 14

Works by composers in Italy:

Busoni:

1907:	*Elegies; An die Jugend*
1910:	*Sonatina #1*
1910-12:	*Fantasia contrapuntistica*
1912:	*Sonatina #2*

Works by composers in the United States:

Ives:

1902-04:	*Ragtime Pieces*
1905:	*Three-Page Sonata*
1901-09:	*Sonata #1*
1911-15:	*Sonata #2, "Concord"*

The following sections will focus upon Prokofiev's treatment of harmony, melody, rhythm, texture, form, and pianistic technique in his Russian-period piano works, in an effort to place these works into historical context.

Harmony in Prokofiev's Russian-period Piano Works

Harmonic practice. Prokofiev's harmonies, even at their most complex, are rooted in the system of functional harmony that was codified by Rameau in 1722 and practiced by major composers until the beginning of the twentieth century. Prokofiev's harmony is derived from tertian harmony with few exceptions. It depends mostly upon triads (major, minor, diminished, and augmented) and seventh chords, although his tertian chords are often disguised by added tones. Chords of the augmented sixth also play an important role, and an occasional quartal chord may be found.

Prokofiev's harmony is tonal. His cadence points are clear, despite the fact that his cadences often finish on unexpected chords or in unexpected keys as the result of abrupt modulations. Often what appear to be distantly related harmonies may be analyzed within the context of functional harmonic progressions, once enharmonic note-spellings and substitutions have been taken into consideration. The following analysis, by P. R. Ashley, of an excerpt from a Prokofiev march shows how one of Prokofiev's complex sequences of chords may be explained in terms of functional harmony (Figure 2.1).[16]

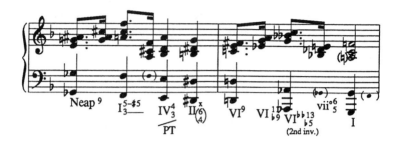

Figure 2.1. Serge Prokofiev, "March," Opus 3 #3, measures 1-4.

Prokofiev, in his autobiography, states that his early experimentation with audacious harmonies was spurred on by a remark made by the eminent composer Serge Taneyev when the eleven-year old Prokofiev showed Taneyev his first completed symphony:

> When we had played the symphony, Taneyev said, "Bravo! Bravo! But the harmonic treatment is a bit simple. Mostly just . . . heh, heh . . . I, IV and V progressions."

> When I got home, I broke into tears and began to rack my brains trying to think up harmonic complexities . . . Only four years later, my harmonic inventions were attracting attention.   And when, eight years later, I played one of my most recent compositions for Taneyev, he muttered, "It seems to have a lot of false notes."[17]

In her theoretical study of Prokofiev's piano music, Ashley has categorized Prokofiev's departures from Western common-practice harmony under the following headings:

a)   Harmonic side-slipping and substitution
b)   Creation of new chords by chromatic
      motion of one or more lines against a pedal point

c) Harmonic elision
d) Parallelism
e) Harmonies based upon unusual scales
f) Unexpected modulations to foreign keys and
    unusual key relationships
g) Chromatic harmony
h) Polychords and superimposed chords
i) Creation of new chords through added
    tones.[18]

a) *Harmonic side-slipping and substitution.* Examples of harmonic side-slipping (use of neighbor chords in place of traditional chords, sometimes effecting a brief transition to a distant key), as well as more common harmonic substitutions, occur frequently in Prokofiev's early piano pieces. As Israel Nestyev points out, the "March," Opus 12 #1, is a revision of an earlier unpublished march, which Prokofiev revised by substituting chords containing altered notes and neighbor chords in place of the traditional harmonies of the original version (as in Figure 2.2).[19] This piece certainly supports the remark once made by Prokofiev's eldest son, that his father "takes music that sounds like other people's music and then Prokofievizes it."[20] Perhaps an analogy could be drawn here with Fauvist techniques in painting, in which familiar subjects are frequently painted with unorthodox colors that substitute for familiar ones.

(a) (cont.)

(b) (cont.)

Figure 2.2. Prokofiev, "March," Opus 12 #1, measures 1-8: (a) original version (1906); and (b) revised version (1913). Reprinted by permission of Boosey and Hawkes, Inc.

Many other examples of side-slipping and substitution may be cited from the early piano pieces.   As Ashley notes, there is an example in the "Jest," Opus 3 #2, of tones being traded between one chord and the next (Figure 2.3).[21]

← displaced ("traded") tones

Figure 2.3. Prokofiev, "Jest," Opus 3 #2, measure 32.

In the "Diabolical Suggestion," Opus 4 #4, the final cadence has an augmented III chord substituting for the dominant. Also, in the "Rigaudon," Opus 12 #3, and in the second piano *Sonata,* we find chords a tritone apart that substitute for more traditional chords a fourth or fifth apart (Figure 2.4).

Figure 2.4. Prokofiev, *Sonata #2,* Opus 14, fourth movement (Vivace), measures 176-179. Reprinted by permission of Boosey and Hawkes, Inc.

b) *Creation of new chords by chromatic motion of one or more lines against a pedal point (oblique chromatic motion).* In the *Four Etudes,* Opus 2, there are a few examples of unorthodox progressions involving oblique motion against pedal points. In the "Diabolical Suggestion," Opus 4 #4; in the *Toccata,* Opus 11; and in the scherzo of the second *Sonata,* Opus 14, this technique comes strongly to the fore (Figures 2.5 and 2.6).

Figure 2.5. Prokofiev, "Diabolical Suggestion," Opus 4 #4, measures 116-118.

Figure 2.6. Prokofiev, *Sonata #2*, Opus 14, second movement (Allegro marcato), measures 25-26. Reprinted by permission of Boosey and Hawkes, Inc.

c) *Harmonic Elision.* The term "harmonic elision" refers to a compositional technique in which a chord normally present within a standard progression in omitted entirely or merely alluded to in passing. This technique does not occur as frequently as do many of Prokofiev's other harmonic procedures, nor is it as easy to identify. A striking example of this technique occurs in the second piano *Sonata*, Opus 14, at measure 19, where the dominant chord is elided, being represented only briefly by the dominant note (Figure 2.7).

Figure 2.7. Prokofiev, *Sonata #2*, Opus 14, first movement (Allegro ma non troppo), measures 19-21. Reprinted by permission of Boosey and Hawkes, Inc.

Perhaps Prokofiev was following a famous precedent from Beethoven's *Sonata,* Opus 109 (second movement), in which the dominant chord is omitted entirely between the chord of V/V and the tonic chord (Figure 2.8).

Figure 2.8. Ludwig van Beethoven, *Sonata,* Opus 109, second movement (Prestissimo), measures 102-105.

d) *Parallelism.* Nestyev observes that Prokofiev had already experimented with parallelism and planed triads in one of his earliest pieces, written in 1902, several years before the publication of his *Sonata,* Opus 1.[22] Prokofiev continued to experiment with parallel intervals and chords in many of his early piano works.

The most striking illustration of this technique of parallelism in Prokofiev's early works is the "Mazurka," Opus 12 #4, in which the right hand moves entirely in parallel fourths, while the left hand moves in counterpoint, also in parallel fourths (Figure 2.9). However, as Ashley points out, this piece is not an experiment in quartal harmony since the implied harmonies are tertian.[23]

Figure 2.9. Prokofiev, "Mazurka," Opus 12 #4, measures 1-3.
Reprinted by permission of Boosey and Hawkes, Inc.

In a similar case, in the first movement of the second *Sonata,* Opus 14 (mm. 95-99), Prokofiev doubles a cadential phrase in parallel fourths without obscuring the underlying triadic harmony (Figure 2.10). Other intervals used in parallel motion in Prokofiev's early piano works include perfect fifths ("Legend," Opus 12 #6, measures 1-4), minor ninths ("Diabolical Suggestion," Opus 4 #4, Figure 2.11), and minor sevenths ("Despair," Opus 4 #3, measures 27-28). Unusual examples of parallel chords include parallel augmented triads and Mm 6/5 chords ("March," Opus 3 #3, Figure 2.12), parallel quartal chord formations (*Sonata #4,* Opus 29, third movement, measures 191-193), and major triads planed over the notes of a whole-tone scale ("Humoresque Scherzo," Opus 12 #4, measures 73-74).

Figure 2.10. Prokofiev, *Sonata #2,* Opus 14, first movement (Allegro ma non troppo), measures 95-97. Reprinted by permission of Boosey and Hawkes, Inc.

Figure 2.11. Prokofiev, "Diabolical Suggestion," Opus 4 #4, measures 56-58.

Figure 2.12. Prokofiev, "March," Opus 3 #3, measures 12-13.

e) *Harmonies based upon unusual scales.*   Prokofiev occasionally ventured outside of the major-minor system in his early works with the use of whole-tone and modal scales. In the first and fourth etudes of his *Four Etudes,* Opus 2, there are whole-tone octave passages that are accompanied by chords derived from the whole-tone scale (Figure 2.13).

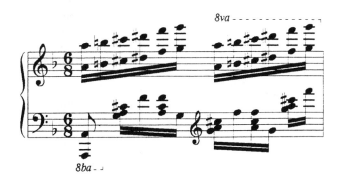

Figure 2.13. Prokofiev, "Etude," Opus 2 #1, measure 71.

The harmonically experimental piece entitled "Despair," Opus 4 #3, has no key signature and contains harmonic progressions that cannot comfortably be placed within any key, although the tonics fall mostly within the whole-tone scale of D (Figure 2.14).[24]

Figure 2.14. Prokofiev, "Despair," Opus 4 #3, measures 9-10.

Modality figures prominently in certain early piano works of Prokofiev. "Story," Opus 3 #1 (Figure 2.15), is primarily a study in modality and chromaticism. The *Toccata,* Opus 11 (Figure 2.16), and the first theme of the first piano *Sonata,* Opus 1, begin in the Aeolian mode (the natural minor scale).

Figure 2.15. Prokofiev, "Story," Opus 3 #1, measures 4-5.

Figure 2.16. Prokofiev, *Toccata,* Opus 11, measures 9-11.

f) *Unexpected modulations to foreign keys and unusual key relationships.* Examples of unexpected modulations to foreign keys and unusual key relationships abound in the early piano works of Prokofiev. "Despair," Opus 4 #3, and the "Diabolical Suggestion," Opus 4 #4, are two works in which modulations are made to tonics that fall within the whole-tone scale. In the "Diabolical Suggestion," particularly, Prokofiev employed the devices of sudden chromatic, enharmonic, and common-chord modulations (Figure 2.17).

Figure 2.17. Prokofiev, "Diabolical Suggestion," Opus 4 #4, measures 28-30.

In his "Legend," Opus 12 #6, Prokofiev frequently employs a technique used by Beethoven that Ashley has dubbed "modulation by fermata"[25] (i.e., beginning freely in a new key after pausing on a chord in the old key [Figure 2.18]).

ppp

Figure 2.18. Prokofiev, "Legend," Opus 12 #6, measures 13-14.
Reprinted by permission of Boosey and Hawkes, Inc.

Prokofiev often experimented, in his early piano pieces, with wide-ranging tonal schemes. The "Etude," Opus 2 #2, to cite one example, begins in the key of E minor and features modulatory excursions to E-flat, G-sharp minor, B minor, G minor, and D minor, before returning to the home key.

g) *Chromatic harmonies (chords with altered tones).* In his use of chromatic chords in the early piano works, Prokofiev went beyond the use of secondary dominants, chords of the augmented sixth, and chords borrowed from the parallel major or minor key. Examples of unusual chromatic chords include an augmented chord built on the flatted fourth scale degree ("Phantom," Opus 3 #4, Figure 2.19); chords based upon the tritone—the *"diabolis in musica"*—(appropriately prominent in the "Diabolical Suggestion," Opus 4 #4, Figure 2.20); and a Neapolitan chord with an added tritone that moves to a dominant ninth chord with a flatted fifth ("Caprice," Opus 12 #5, Figure 2.21).

Figures 2.19, 2.20, 2.21. Chromatic harmonies in Prokofiev's "Phantom," Opus 3 #4, measures 3-4; "Diabolical Suggestion," Opus 4 #4, measure 6; and "Caprice," Opus 12 #5, measures 102-103.

Figure 2.21 reprinted by permission of Boosey and Hawkes, Inc.

h) *Superimposed chords and bitonality.* In the early piano works, Prokofiev often used superimposed chords, sometimes within a single key, sometimes bitonally. He also made occasional use of bitonal counterpoint.

In the "Mazurka," Opus 3 #3, the *Toccata,* Opus 11, and most of Prokofiev's humorous pieces, there are many polychords. In the "Diabolical Suggestion" and in the second *Sonata,* there are several bitonal passages. In the second *Sonata,* there are also striking examples of polytonality produced by the combination of two or more themes in different keys (Figure 2.22).

Figure 2.22. Prokofiev, *Sonata #2,* Opus 14, fourth movement (Vivace), measures 97-98. Reprinted by permission of Boosey and Hawkes, Inc.

In the third "Sarcasm," Prokofiev uses two key signatures simultaneously: three sharps in the right hand against five flats in the left (Figure 2.23).

Figure 2.23. Prokofiev, "Sarcasm," Opus 17 #3, measures 3-4. Used with the permission of G. Schirmer, Inc., New York (ASCAP) on behalf of RAIS (Russia).

    i) ***Chords with added tones.*** Often Prokofiev adds major or minor seconds to tertian chords in individual ways. This gives an added dissonant bite or spice to these chords, often adding an overtone of wit or irony to the music's character (Figures 2.24 and 2.25).

Figure 2.24 and 2.25. Prokofiev, *Sonata #2,* Opus 14, fourth movement (Vivace), measures 158-159; and measures 87-88. Reprinted by permission of Boosey and Hawkes, Inc.

    Prokofiev also exploits chords of the added tritone in the introductory section of the "Diabolical Suggestion," Opus 4 #4 (see Figure 2.20).

Historical context. According to anecdote, Anatole Liadov, professor of harmony at the St. Petersburg Conservatory, once told his student Prokofiev, "If you want to write modern music, go study with Debussy or Strauss."[26] Prokofiev must have taken the remark seriously, at least insofar as he and his friend and fellow composer, Miaskovsky, spent many hours together exploring the music of Debussy, Strauss, Scriabin, and Reger.

Many of Prokofiev's harmonic techniques may have been derived from developments in contemporary French music. Debussy had already incorporated sophisticated parallelisms ("La soirée dans Grenade," from *Estampes,* 1903); whole-tone scales ("Pagodes," from *Estampes,* 1903); and chord-streams ("Reflets dans l'eau, from *Images,* Book I, 1905) into his piano music by the time Prokofiev began to publish his piano works. Debussy used parallel triads with added tones in 1907 in Book II of his *Images* ("Et la lune descend sur la temple qui fut") and had adopted complex polytonal combinations by the time of the second book of *Préludes* ("Feux d'artifice," 1913). Several years before Prokofiev published his *Sonata, Opus 1,* Ravel had employed polychords and polytonality (*Jeux d'eau,* 1901), and Satie had explored many modal possibilities following the precedent set by Chopin.

In Russia and other parts of Europe, harmonic experiments with far-reaching consequences were occurring during the years 1906-1917, when Prokofiev was writing his early works. Composers during this period were questioning such well-established harmonic foundations as tonality and tertian harmony.

In Russia, Scriabin was experimenting with chord progressions and key relationships a tritone apart by 1907 (*Sonata #5*), with exotic chord formations by 1911 (*Sonata #6*), and with melodies doubled in major ninths in 1912 (*Etude, Opus 65 #1*). In his late sonatas, Scriabin ventured into a realm of obscured tonality.

In Vienna, in 1909, Schoenberg wrote his first atonal pieces: the *Drei Klavierstücke, Opus 11.* Also, in Vienna in 1908, Berg wrote his only major piano work—the *Sonata, Opus 1*—in a post-Wagnerian chromatic idiom.

In Hungary, in 1908, Bartók was experimenting with bitonality using different key signatures for the right and left hands (4 sharps/4 flats) in his first "Bagatelle," Opus 6 #1. In the *Bagatelles, Opus 6,* he also experimented with parallel quartal chords and chords having added seconds (Opus 6 #11), chords based upon exotic scales (Opus 6 #14), parallel minor sevenths (Opus 6 #9), and neighbor chords that substitute for other chords (Opus 6 #14). In the "Dirge," Opus 8B #1 (1908), he experimented with polychords, chords built from a perfect fourth plus a tritone, and parallel diminished-seventh chords. In the *Sketches,* Opus 9B (1908-1910), there are examples of unusual enharmonic modulations (Opus 9B #1), bitonal counterpoint (Opus 9B #2), and cluster chords (Opus 9B #5). The "Dirge," Opus 9A #3, has a left-hand part that moves almost entirely in parallel fifths. In the *Suite,* Opus 14, Bartók employs tritone relationships in the opening of the first movement and parallel chords with added tones in the scherzo. Many progressions in Bartók's early works do not fit comfortably into any key and seem to wander freely between unrelated keys.

In Italy, Busoni's experiments included chord progressions a tritone apart, polychords, tonal fluctuations, and progressions based upon the whole-tone scale in the first two of his *Elegies* (1907). The seventh of his *Elegies,* "Berceuse" (1909), features polytonal passages and chords built from a tritone plus a perfect fourth.

In the United States, in the early part of the twentieth century, Ives developed a unique idiom, incorporating bitonality, parallelism, clusters, and chords with added tones into his harmonic language.

Although Prokofiev learned from his predecessors and contemporaries, he probably deserves credit as an innovator for creating, in 1908, the first piano piece in which voices are doubled entirely in parallel fourths. The "Mazurka," Opus 12 #4 (1908), has melodies doubled in parallel fourths in the right hand moving in counterpoint against melodies doubled in parallel fourths in the left hand. This work anticipates Debussy's "Etude pour les quartes" (1915) by seven years.

Prokofiev also deserves credit for elevating the technique of harmonic side-slipping (substitution) into a pervasive principle of composition. Although Bartók used this principle in 1908 ("Bagatelle," Opus 6 #14, ["Ma mie qui danse"]), he used it only briefly, soon moving on to different keys and different techniques. Prokofiev, in the "March," Opus 3 #3, and the finale of the second *Sonata,* Opus 14 (1912), keeps his tonal centers stable while employing the harmonic side-slipping technique for long periods of time.

Prokofiev also took the principle of creating new chords by oblique chromatic motion and employed it to an unprecedented extent. The "Diabolical Suggestion," the scherzo of the second *Sonata,* and the *Toccata* employ this technique with a thoroughness, rhythmic aggressiveness, and emphasis on dissonance that set them far apart from Liszt's "Feux follets," a piece that also employs this technique. In his use of chord progressions that do not fit comfortably into any key, Prokofiev, in his early years, was equalled in daring by very few composers, notably Bartók, Scriabin, Ives, and Schoenberg. In his use of parallelisms, whole-tone scales, modality, bitonality, and chords with various added tones, the young Prokofiev showed himself to be in tune with most of the advanced harmonic practices of his contemporaries.

Melody in Prokofiev's Russian-period Piano Works

Melodic practice. Although Prokofiev's melodies in the early piano works are tonal, they often display characteristics that depart significantly from melodies of previous centuries. In addition, when his melodies are conventional, they are usually harmonized in unconventional ways.

Given Prokofiev's neo-Classic and neo-Romantic aesthetic principles, it is not surprising that the melodic material employed by Prokofiev in any given situation depends upon its structural role ("A" theme, "B" theme, transition, development, etc.); functions interdependently with the other musical elements; and shows the influence of affective or imaginative considerations. In Prokofiev's more energetic movements, his melodies tend to have many leaps and frequently require crossing of the hands (Figure 2.26).

Figure 2.26. Prokofiev, *Sonata #2,* Opus 14, fourth movement (Vivace), measures 17-21.
Reprinted by permission of Boosey and Hawkes, Inc.

His slower, more serious melodies usually move primarily by step or chromatically (Figure 2.27).

Figure 2.27. Prokofiev, *Sonata #2*, Opus 14, first movement (Allegro ma non troppo), measures 253-260. Reprinted by permission of Boosey and Hawkes, Inc.

a) *Melodic side-slipping and displacement.* As Kinsey remarks in his discussion of Prokofiev's piano sonatas, devices that appear frequently in Prokofiev's early melodies include side-slipping (substitution of a neighbor tone for an expected tone), use of other foreign tones, and distortion by octave displacement, devices that are often coupled with abrupt, unexpected leaps.[27] These devices help to create two related types of melody, identified by Ashley, that have two distinctly different purposes:

1)   the "amusing" tune, dependent frequently upon substituted tones or "wrong notes," generally a half-step off, and on awkward leaps and bizarre or primitive rhythms.

2)   the angular, serious melody, related in structure to the amusing tune, but through subtle means (dynamics, instrument, characteristic harmonies) made more tragic.[28]

An example of the amusing Prokofiev tune is the theme of the development section in the finale of the second piano *Sonata* (Figure 2.28). The distortion of conventional leaps of octaves or fifths creates a comic effect in much the same way as the distortion of familiar shapes in a fun-house mirror provides us with amusement.

Figure 2.28. Prokofiev, *Sonata #2*, Opus 14, fourth movement (Vivace), measures 176-178. Reprinted by permission of Boosey and Hawkes, Inc.

An example of the angular, serious melody is the opening theme of the first of the *Visions fugitives* (Figure 2.29):

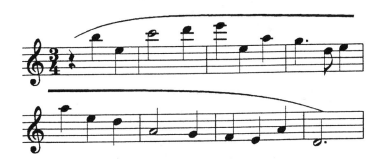

Figure 2.29. Prokofiev, "Vision fugitive," Opus 22 #1, measures 1-8. Reprinted by permission of Boosey and Hawkes, Inc.

By stretching traditional intervallic relationships, Prokofiev sometimes extended the range of nonessential tones. Ashley notes that, in the "March," Opus 3 #3, Prokofiev allows notes that lie halfway between large leaps to function as passing tones (Figure 2.30).[29]

Figure 2.30. Prokofiev, "March," Opus 3 #3, measure 12.

As well, Ashley observes that, in "Elan," Opus 4 #2, Prokofiev allows rather distant tones to function as neighbor tones (Figure 2.31).[30]

Figure 2.31. Prokofiev, "Elan," Opus 4 #2, measure 8.

   b) *Melodies based upon unusual scales.*   Sometimes unusual scales, especially modal or whole-tone scales, provide the raw material for unusual Prokofiev melodies. In the opening of Prokofiev's "Etude," Opus 2 #3, the pianist's right hand weaves arabesques in the Phrygian mode. In the first two *Sonatas*, the opening themes are based upon the natural minor scale (Figure 2.32).

Figure 2.32. Prokofiev, *Sonata #1,* Opus 1, measures 5-6.

Prokofiev uses the whole-tone scale melodically in the "Etudes," Opus 2 #1 and Opus 2 #4; and the "Humoresque Scherzo," Opus 12 #9. The whole-tone scale also underlies much of the melodic material of "Despair," Opus 4 #3 (Figure 2.33).

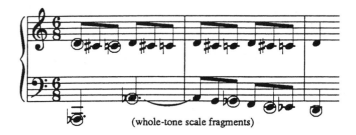

(whole-tone scale fragments)

Figure 2.33. Prokofiev, "Despair," Opus 4 #3, measures 3-5.

c) *Motivic melody and repeated-note melody.* Prokofiev often eschews lyricism and long-breathed themes in favor of terse motivic writing. His emphasis on motivic melody probably reflects his admiration for Beethoven.

Prokofiev's *Toccata,* Opus 11, is based almost exclusively on short motives derived from repeated notes, the chromatic scale, and the arpeggiated minor triad (Figure 2.34).

Figure 2.34. Prokofiev, *Toccata,* Opus 11, measures 24-26.

This piece generates much of its energy from a single note (i.e., the repeated tonic note "D"). Tension is further created in this piece by melodic stress on repeated leading-tones as well as the repeated tonic (Figure 2.35).

Figure 2.35. Prokofiev, *Toccata,* Opus 11, measures 71-72.

Historical context. Melodically, Prokofiev in his first period was an innovative composer who borrowed techniques from the past and from his contemporaries and gave them his own personal stamp. A brief survey of melodic developments in music by Prokofiev's contemporaries will help to place the young Prokofiev's melodic practice in historical perspective.

By the early twentieth century, Western music had been enriched by melodic material outside of the major-minor system.

Whole-tone melody appeared in Russian music as early as Glinka's opera *Russlan and Ludmilla* (1842), and later became an integral element in many of Debussy's works, for example *L'isle joyeuse* (1904). Pentatonic melody was used to evoke the exotic East in Debussy's "Pagodes" (from *Estampes*, 1903). Modal melodies, an integral part of European folk-music, were restored to Western music by nationalist composers as early as Chopin. Atonal melody was an experimental feature of Schoenberg's *Drei Klavierstücke*, Opus 11 (1908). In Hungary, in the *Bagatelles*, Opus 14 (1908), Bartók experimented with melodies that freely wander among distantly related keys, melodies that outline quartal or quintal chords, melodies with wrong notes (substituted tones), and melodies that employ octave displacement. In the *Allegro barbaro* (1911), Bartók experimented with primitivist melody. Ives, working in the United States in isolation from his European contemporaries, experimented during this period with melodic substitution and tonally wandering melody. Prokofiev employed all of these techniques in his early piano works with the exception of atonal melody, pentatonic melody, and melody that outlines quartal and quintal chords.

Although Bartók in his *Bagatelles* (1908) may have anticipated Prokofiev in the use of tonally wandering melody, melody with substituted tones, and amusing melodic parody, Prokofiev adopted these techniques and developed them to the extent that they became trademarks of his style. In the same way as we associate atonality with Schoenberg rather than Liszt (despite Liszt's prophetic *Bagatelle Without Tonality*), so we tend to think particularly of melodic substitution and melodic parody as Prokofiev techniques. One of the main reasons why we tend to have strong associations with the music of Prokofiev is the fact that Prokofiev often wrote clear-cut, memorable themes that, like Classical themes, were meant to be easily recognizable upon their recurrence.

Although Bartók's primitivistic *Allegro barbaro* (1911) briefly anticipated Prokofiev's turn to primitivist melody in the *Toccata* (1912), Prokofiev's *Toccata* nevertheless broke new ground melodically. The reduction of melodic interest at the opening of a piece to a single drumming repetition of the tonic and the use of that single note as a focal point from which other terse motives are generated were unprecedented ideas in the year 1912.

Rhythm and Meter in Prokofiev's Russian-period Piano Works

Rhythmic techniques. In Prokofiev's Russian-period piano works, the rhythmic patterns are rarely in themselves innovative. However, the rhythmic element plays a vital role in the musical characterization of these early works. The following rhythmic devices found in Prokofiev's early piano pieces are either innovative or sufficiently prominent to be considered integral to his early style.

a) *Perpetual motion (motoric rhythm).* The perpetual motion principle is the rhythmic principle found most often in Prokofiev's early piano works. Prokofiev's admiration for Beethoven is evident in his obsession with perpetual motion, one of the hallmarks of Beethoven's second style-period. Perhaps the influence is also to be found of certain motoric preludes of Chopin and Bach or of certain etudes of Chopin and Liszt.

Examples of perpetual motion abound in Prokofiev's early works for piano, beginning with Opus 2. Each of the *Four Etudes, Opus 2*, is a study in perpetual rhythmic motion (Figure 2.36).

Figure 2.36. Prokofiev, "Etude", Opus 2 #1, measures 1-2.

Also, each of Prokofiev's early collections of piano pieces contains at least one perpetual motion exercise (Figure 2.37).

Figure 2.37. Prokofiev, "Scherzo," Opus 12 #10, measures 5-8.
Reprinted by permission of Boosey and Hawkes, Inc.

Of all of Prokofiev's early piano works, however, it is the *Toccata*, Opus 11, that most powerfully illustrates the principle of perpetual motion. This piece is a *tour de force* of rhythmic obsession. It is dominated by a sixteenth-note rhythm pursued with almost primitive insistence. From its opening measure until the final glissando, the sixteenth-note pulsation hardly ever relents (see Figures 2.34 and 2.35).

The second piano *Sonata,* Opus 14, may be used to illustrate four different ways in which Prokofiev combines perpetual rhythmic motion with melody:

1)   perpetual motion and a freely changing melody
     (Figure 2.38 a);

2)   perpetual motion and a strictly repeating, lyrical melodic
     pattern, creating an ostinato (Figure 2.38 b);

3)   perpetual motion and a repeated note or chord, creating
     a rhythmic ostinato (Figure 2.38 c);

4)   perpetual motion and a strictly repeating, angular
     melody, creating a *stile mécanique* pattern
     (a mechanistic ostinato [Figure 2.38 d and e]).

Figure 2.38 (a-e). Prokofiev, Ostinato and *stile-mécanique* figures from the *Sonata #2*, Opus 14. Reprinted by permission of Boosey and Hawkes, Inc.

b) ***Unusual meters.*** Prokofiev experimented occasionally with unusual meters in his early piano pieces. The two primary examples are the "Phantom," Opus 3 #4, which is in 5/8 meter (Figure 2.39), and the "Etude," Opus 2 #3, in which the right hand weaves arabesques in 18/16 meter while the left hand accompanies in 4/4 meter (Figure 2.40).

Figures 2.39 and 2.40. Unusual meters in Prokofiev's "Phantom," Opus 3 #4, measures 1-3; and "Etude," Opus 2 #3, measure 1.

In the second *Sonata,* Prokofiev casts the closing theme of the second movement in the unusual meter of 7/8 (Figure 2.41).

Figure 2.41. Prokofiev, *Sonata #2*, Opus 14, third movement (Andante), measures 54-55. Reprinted by permission of Boosey and Hawkes, Inc.

c) *Polyrhythms, polymeter, and frequently changing meters (multimeter).* Prokofiev experimented occasionally with the techniques of polyrhythm and polymeter in his early piano pieces. In the "Etude," Opus 2 #2, he combines 3/4 meter in the left hand with 6/8 meter in the right hand. In the third etude of Opus 2, he combines 18/16 meter in the right hand with 4/4 meter in the left; this creates polyrhythms of nine notes against four, which he later changes to more complicated polyrhythms of nine notes against five. In the last "Vision fugitive," the right hand begins in 9/8 against 3/4 in the left. In the finale of the second *Sonata*, Prokofiev adds rhythmic excitement to the development by polymetric combination of two themes: the transition theme in 6/8 and the second subject ostinato in 2/4 (Figure 2.42).

Figure 2.42. Polymetric combination of themes in Prokofiev's *Sonata #2*, Opus 14, fourth movement (Vivace), measures 97-98. Reprinted by permission of Boosey and Hawkes, Inc.

In the fifth "Sarcasm," Prokofiev utilized frequently changing meters (multimeter). This is the only piano piece where he employed this technique throughout the entire piece.

Figure 2.43. Prokofiev, "Sarcasm," Opus 17 #5, measures 1-4. Used with the permission of G. Schirmer, Inc., New York (ASCAP) on behalf of RAIS (Russia).

d) *Accents and syncopation.* Prokofiev's rhythms are spiced often with strong accents and sforzandi and occasionally with syncopated accents or offbeat rhythms. These devices are reminiscent of Beethoven's rhythmic surprises. Syncopation figures prominently in the opening of the "Sarcasm," Opus 17 #5 (Figure 2.44).

Figure 2.44. Prokofiev, "Sarcasm," Opus 17 #5, measures 1-2. Used with the permission of G. Schirmer, Inc., New York (ASCAP) on behalf of RAIS (Russia).

Offbeat chords, strong accents, and sforzandi are prominent in the "Diabolical Suggestion," Opus 4 #4 (Figure 2.45).

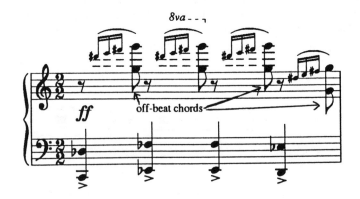

Figure 2.45. Prokofiev, "Diabolical Suggestion," Opus 4 #4, measure 95.

Historical context. The rhythms in Prokofiev's Russian-period piano music are not on the whole innovative. Most could be found in the Classical period. They are always metrical, are usually unsyncopated, and rarely use note-values smaller than a sixteenthnote. The influence of Beethoven has already been mentioned in the perpetual motion pieces, the sforzandi, and the occasional syncopations. Rhythmically, the scherzo and tarantella finale of the second *Sonata* may have been influenced by the corresponding movements in Beethoven's *Sonata* in E-flat, Opus 31 #3.

Some sophisticated rhythmic devices were probably borrowed by Prokofiev from Romantic and contemporary composers. Chopin had introduced many new polyrhythmic combinations spanning one or many beats in a measure. Chopin also introduced polymetric combinations of 6/8 and 3/4 in his *Waltz*, Opus 42, and *Scherzo*, Opus 54. Unusual polyrhythmic and polymetric combinations were used in Romantic compositions from Schumann's *Carnaval* and *Kreisleriana* to Scriabin's sonatas and etudes.

Quintuple, septuple, and other unusual meters were rare until the twentieth century. Isolated examples can be found in the works of Chopin, Tschaikovsky, Brahms, and Rimsky-Korsakov, however.

In the early twentieth century, composers began to experiment more often with unusual meters. Scriabin used 5/8 meter for part of the introduction to his fifth *Sonata* (1907), and 15/8 for his "Prelude," Opus 11 #14. Bartók employed frequently changing meters including 7/8, 5/8, and 10/16 in the "Dirge," Opus 8B #2 (1909), a piece that also contains the complex polymetric combination of 4/4 and 3/4. In the "Sketch," Opus 9 #7 (1910), Bartók even experimented with measures of additive meter, e.g. $\frac{6+2}{8}$, a device Prokofiev encountered in Medtner's *Fairy Tales*, Opus 8.[31] Ives's "*Concord*" *Sonata* contains frequent meter changes and measures of irregular meter, as well as sections of unmeasured rhythm.

Prokofiev's choice of 5/8 meter for the "Phantom," Opus 3 #4 (1911) appears to have been the first use of this meter for an entire piece. Prokofiev's use of 7/8 meter for an entire theme in the second *Sonata* is probably also original. His combination of 18/16 in the right hand with 4/4 in the left hand ("Etude," Opus 2 #3, 1909) is almost certainly original.

The emancipation of meter in the early twentieth century is often credited to Stravinsky. Prokofiev's use of frequently changing meter in the fifth "Sarcasm" may reflect the impact of Stravinsky's *Rite of Spring* (1913). Prokofiev rejected certain contemporary rhythmic developments and was probably unaware of others. Debussy's fluidity of rhythm was rejected out-of-hand by Prokofiev, who preferred the antithesis: precise, sharply defined rhythm. Ragtime syncopation, adopted by Debussy, Ives, and Satie on occasion, figures briefly in Prokofiev's sixth *Sonata* but never in his early piano works. Unmeasured rhythm, as found in Ives's *"Concord" Sonata* (1911-15), is not found in Prokofiev's piano works.

In the elevation of perpetual motion (motoric rhythm) to a dominant position as a rhythmic principle in his early works, Prokofiev followed a path that diverged from the paths of most of his contemporaries but that nevertheless had an impact upon twentieth-century music. In the *Toccata,* Opus 11, Prokofiev deserves credit for sustaining a motoric rhythmic drive with a relentlessness that equalled or surpassed that of any previous composition.

Texture in Prokofiev's Russian-period Piano Works

Practice. Prokofiev helped to pioneer the twentieth-century return to clear, contrapuntal writing. In his work, counterpoint occupies a position at least as important as that occupied by homophony.

Boris de Schloezer has written, concerning Prokofiev's textures:

> Horizontal writing is dominant with him: his extremely clear polyphonic web has no great complexity; and even when he lapses into homophony and his music becomes an accompanied melody, one still gets a very clear impression that the composer only considers each instant's sonority in its relation to those which precede and follow it and never for itself.[32]

The validity of this argument is borne out by the fact that many of Prokofiev's chords are either created by contrapuntal lines or have strong linear connections. It is also true that Prokofiev did not frequently rely upon hymn-tune or broken-chord homophony, nor did he isolate sonorities in the way that Debussy or Schoenberg did. On the other hand, like any composer who writes functional harmony, Prokofiev considers his chords as individual sonorities that function interdependently within a system of functional harmonic relationships. In Prokofiev's music, functional harmony provides a stabilizing vertical framework that interacts with the strong horizontal forces of voice-leading and dissonance resolution. Also, in certain passages, Prokofiev leaps from chord to chord, thereby emphasizing the separateness of each chord rather than the contrapuntal connections between successive chords (Figure 2.46).

Figure 2.46. Prokofiev, "Jest," Opus 3 #2, measures 1-2.

In the most homophonic passages in Prokofiev's early piano pieces, there are either solid chords or else the left hand supplies a simple broken-chord accompaniment to a melody in the right hand. These broken-chord accompaniments consist of either neo-Mozartian Alberti-bass patterns (fourth *Sonata,* finale, "A" theme, Figure 2.47) or neo-Romantic arpeggio patterns (second *Sonata,* first movement, "B" theme, Figure 2.48).

Figure 2.47. Accompaniment figure in Prokofiev's *Sonata #4,* Opus 29, third movement (Vivace), measures 10-13. Reprinted by permission of Boosey and Hawkes, Inc.

Figure 2.48. Accompaniment figure in Prokofiev's *Sonata #2*, Opus 14,
first movement (Allegro ma non troppo), measures 72-75.
Reprinted by permission of Boosey and Hawkes, Inc.

At the other end of the counterpoint-homophony scale, in his most academically contrapuntal sections, Prokofiev's early music employs the devices of augmentation, imitation, stretto, mirroring, and contrapuntal combination of themes. In the *Toccata,* Opus 11, at a climactic point, Prokofiev combines a bare broken-triad pattern in one voice with its augmentation in another voice (Figure 2.49), while at the end of the fifteenth "Vision fugitive," he combines a motive with both its augmentation and its double augmentation.

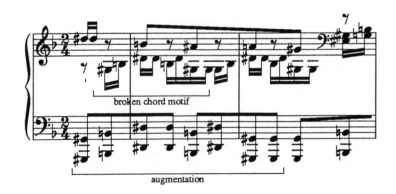

Figure 2.49. Prokofiev, *Toccata,* Opus 11, measures 132-134.

In the development section of the first movement of the second *Sonata*, Prokofiev skillfully combines material from three different themes: the second subject (rhythmically altered from triple meter to duple), plus two different ostinato figures taken from the bridge between the first and second subject groups (Figure 2.50).

Figure 2.50. Prokofiev, *Sonata #2,* Opus 14, first movement (Allegro ma non troppo), measures 143-147. Reprinted by permission of Boosey and Hawkes, Inc.

In his early piano works, Prokofiev's textures most often, however, occupy a middle-ground between pure counterpoint and pure homophony. The voices, although rhythmically independent, are rarely equal. Often, the soprano has the tune, while the bass-line defines the harmonic function and the middle voices supply counter-melodies that complete the harmony, create contrapuntal interest, and provide forward movement rhythmically (Figure 2.51).

Figure 2.51. Prokofiev, "Story," Opus 3 #1, measures 4-5.

At other times, one or more voices will carry an ostinato, creating contrapuntal interest within an otherwise homophonic texture (Figure 2.52).

Figure 2.52. Prokofiev, "Phantom," Opus 3 #4, measures 3-6.

At still other times, Prokofiev employs single or double pedal points. Both the first *Sonata* (development section), and the second *Sonata* ("A" theme of the third movement), feature double pedal points (Figure 2.53).

Figure 2.53. Prokofiev, *Sonata #2*, Opus 14, third movement (Andante), measures 2-4.
Reprinted by permission of Boosey and Hawkes, Inc.

Historical context. Prokofiev's use of contrapuntal texture and modernized Alberti-bass patterns in his early piano pieces deserves recognition. At a time when many late-Romantic composers were still relying upon arpeggio accompaniments or thickly textured counterpoint, Prokofiev was helping, in some of his early piano works, to effect a return to Classical clarity of texture and thinly textured counterpoint. Prokofiev helped to establish the importance of the ostinato as a textural device in twentieth-century music. In "Despair," Opus 4 #3, Prokofiev took a three-note melodic ostinato figure, and repeated it from beginning to end, while introducing a variety of other ideas in counterpoint; this piece could almost be considered a modernized Baroque ground. In his second *Sonata,* Prokofiev also used repeated-interval and repeated-chord ostinatos, techniques that Bartók had anticipated by only a few years, in his *Bagatelles,* Opus 6 (1908).

Form in Prokofiev's Russian-period Piano Works

Formal practice. For the piano pieces of his Russian period, Prokofiev did not invent new forms. His short pieces employ primarily ABA or rondo structures, and his large structures are cast in sonata or rondo forms. Prokofiev once expressed his satisfaction with traditional forms in the following statement:

> In that field [instrumental or symphonic music], I am well content with the forms already perfected. I want nothing better, nothing more flexible or more complete, than the sonata form, which contains everything necessary to my structural purposes.[33]

Prokofiev's treatment of form in his early sonatas merits further study for two important reasons. First, the sonata form was the foundation of his instrumental writing. Secondly, Prokofiev was a master of the piano sonata; his nine piano sonatas could well be considered the most important set of piano sonatas since Beethoven.[34]

Prokofiev's first *Sonata* is a single sonata-allegro movement, not a Lisztian condensation of several movements into one. It lacks the sharp contrast of themes that mark the best sonata-allegro movements. Originally, Prokofiev intended it to be the first movement of a four-movement sonata, but he chose to abandon work on the other movements.   The second *Sonata* shows the influence of neo-Classicism, especially in its scherzo and finale.   Using both the individual musical language that he had developed through experimentation in smaller-scale works, and the large-scale framework of the Classical piano sonata, Prokofiev was able to create a piano sonata that was, at the same time, innovative as well as highly successful.

The first movement and finale of the second piano *Sonata* feature musical devices that were to become trademarks of Prokofiev's style, including modal or tonally wandering themes, abrupt modulations via sequences, and frequent ostinatos.   There are two striking formal experiments in the first movement: the introduction of a second subject in 3/4 meter within a movement in 2/4 meter and the contrapuntal combination of three thematic ideas in the development.

This sonata, incidentally, is cyclic.   The second subject of the opening movement returns in the development of the finale, thus reinforcing the underlying unity between the first and last movements.

The third *Sonata,* Opus 28, like the first, is a one-movement work.   In this sonata, however, differentiation of themes is intensified by the use of contrasting tempos and meters.   Three important formal elements are the extended introduction beginning on the dominant, the use of pervasive motivic development, and the absence of the second subject in the recapitulation.

The fourth *Sonata,* Opus 29, is a formally conventional three-movement work.   The second movement develops its principal theme in various canons including canon in inversion.   The third movement, a rondo, features strongly differentiated themes and abrupt modulations by sequence.

Historical context.   Prokofiev was not innovative in his formal designs.   However, as Kinsey notes, he helped to pioneer the twentieth-century return to Classical clarity and simplicity of formal design.[35]   His second *Sonata* could be considered the first piano sonata to show a strong influence of neo-Classicism.

Most of Prokofiev's more adventuresome formal techniques were borrowed from past masters.   Prokofiev's choice of different meters for first and second subjects (second *Sonata,* first movement) was unorthodox but not unprecedented (cf. Beethoven's *Sonata,* Opus 109, first movement; and Liszt's *Sonata* in B minor).

Cyclic form, used in the second *Sonata*, is a feature of many nineteenth-century works. Development by changing the meter of a theme was often a part of Liszt's technique of transformation of themes. Both Scriabin in his *Sonata-Fantasy,* Opus 19, and Liszt in the B-minor *Sonata* had contrapuntally combined elements of themes, although these were not bitonal combinations like those in Prokofiev's second *Sonata.* Transition sections featuring abruptly modulating sequences (Figure 2.54) appear to show the influence of Beethoven's second-period works.

transition section, featuring rapidly-modulating sequence

Figure 2.54. Prokofiev, *Sonata #2,* Opus 14, first movement (Allegro ma non troppo), measures 32-43. Reprinted by permission of Boosey and Hawkes, Inc.

Bitonal combinations of themes (see Figure 2.22) appear to be original contributions by Prokofiev to the sonata-allegro movement. The use of a bitonal theme in a sonata (in the slow movement of Prokofiev's second *Sonata,* measures 22-25) was also a forward-looking experiment in 1912.

Pianistic Technique in Prokofiev's Russian-period Piano Music

    Practice.   Being in possession of a virtuoso technique, Prokofiev did not shy away from including formidable technical difficulties in his early piano works. His *Four Etudes*, Opus 2, contain difficult passages based upon octaves, thirds, and sweeping arpeggios (Opus 2 #1); scales (Opus 2 #2); counterpoint within a single hand, requiring rapid changes of hand position (Opus 2 #3); and broken-octave bass and rapid hand-crossing (Opus 2 #4). Rapid hand-crossing and rapid leaps are frequently employed techniques in Prokofiev's early piano works (Figures 2.55 and 2.56).

hand-crossing

Figures 2.55. and 2.56. Prokofiev, *Sonata #2*, Opus 14, second movement, measures 13-14; and Prokofiev, "Scherzo," Opus 12 #10, measures 165-168.
Reprinted by permission of Boosey and Hawkes, Inc.

Glissandi on the white keys also supply an exciting splash of bravura to both the "Diabolical Suggestion" and the *Toccata,* and a touch of delicacy in the "Prelude," Opus 12 #7 (Figure 2.57).

Figure 2.57. Prokofiev, "Prelude," Opus 12 #7, measures 37-38.
Reprinted by permission of Boosey and Hawkes, Inc.

Historical context. Whereas none of the pianistic techniques mentioned above were invented by Prokofiev, he deserves credit for employing the technique of rapid hand-crossing that had remained largely unused by the major composers of the Romantic period (Liszt's "Un sospiro" being a notable exception). Prokofiev's hand-crossing passages do not quite require the agility of Domenico Scarlatti's most infamously difficult passages, yet they are frequently more difficult than those of Beethoven and Mozart.

Although avant-garde techniques such as Schoenberg's harmonics and the tone clusters of Ives and Cowell do not appear in his early works, the young Prokofiev nevertheless merits special mention for the creation of the first expressionistic toccata, i.e., the *Toccata,* Opus 11. This piece contains formidable technical difficulties and requires tremendous endurance.

The Foreign Period (1918-1935)

Biographical Notes

Prokofiev spent the years 1918-1935 for the most part in the United States and France; hence, these years are generally referred to by biographers as Prokofiev's "foreign period."

In 1918, Prokofiev left Russia for the United States, travelling via Japan and Honolulu, and arriving first in San Francisco. While in the United States, Prokofiev divided his time mainly between New York and Chicago. Despite some initial successes, his attempts at American recognition were beset with problems and disappointments. Both his playing and his compositions met with violently mixed reactions from critics and from the public.

Prokofiev spent the years 1920 and 1921 alternating between France and North America. In 1920, after a concert tour of Canada, Prokofiev visited Paris, where he met Ravel. In May 1921, Prokofiev's ballet *The Buffoon* had its successful premiere in Paris. Prokofiev also arranged for the American premiere of his opera *Love for Three Oranges,* which, after several postponements and a threatened lawsuit, became the pride of the Chicago musical scene in the Fall of 1921.

In 1922, Prokofiev returned to Europe, arriving first in Paris. He rented a house temporarily in the Bavarian village of Ettal before settling in Paris in 1923. During his Paris years (1923-1936), he had several works premiered in Paris and in the USSR (including the second *Symphony* and the third piano *Concerto*) with varying degrees of success and failure. During these years, Prokofiev also continued to tour as a concert artist.

While in Paris, Prokofiev numbered among his friends and colleagues the conductor Serge Koussevitsky and those composers currently favored by the Parisian public, namely Igor Stravinsky and the group of French composers who called themselves *Les Six.*[36] Although Prokofiev maintained rather uneasy relationships with his rivals, the works of this period reflect the influence of his fellow composers as he attempted to satisfy the fashionable tastes of contemporary Parisian audiences.

His disappointments continued to outweigh his successes, however, in Paris as well as in the United States. By contrast, the welcome he received and the warm reception of his music in the

Soviet Union as he visited there several times during the years 1927 to 1935 were sufficient to convince him to conclude his foreign-period wanderings and return to his native land.

Style in Prokofiev's Foreign-period Piano Works

The piano music of Prokofiev's foreign period includes the following works:

Opus 31, *Tales of the Old Grandmother,* four pieces, 1918
Opus 32, *Four Pieces,* "Dance," "Minuet," "Gavotte," "Waltz," 1918
Opus 38, *Sonata #5,* 1923 (later revised as Opus 135, without significant stylistic changes)
Opus 45, *Choses en soi, (Things in Themselves),* two pieces, 1928
Opus 54, *Two Sonatinas,* E minor and G, 1931-1932.
Opus 59, *Three Pieces,* 1933-1934: "Promenade," "Landscape," "Sonatina pastorale"
Opus 62, *Pensées,* three pieces, 1933-1934
Opus 65, *Music for Children,* twelve pieces, 1935

Although the *Tales of the Old Grandmother,* Opus 31, and the *Four Pieces,* Opus 32, were written and published outside of Russia, stylistically they have more in common with the works of Prokofiev's Russian period. Beginning with the fifth *Sonata,* however, we find a significant change in style lasting up through the *Pensées,* Opus 62. The *Music for Children,* Opus 65, a pedagogical work, does not figure significantly in a historical study of Prokofiev's style.

In the piano works of his foreign period, Prokofiev aimed toward a neo-Classical aesthetic, one that, as Kinsey points out, closely approached Stravinsky's aesthetic of emotional coolness and objectivity.[37] The absence of strong programmatic associations is evident in the choice of titles, *Things in Themselves* (a concept from Kantian philosophy) being a world apart from "Diabolical Suggestion" or "Phantom." This change in aesthetic is marked by corresponding changes in Prokofiev's handling of musical elements.

Harmony in Prokofiev's Foreign-period Piano Works

Harmonic practice. Prokofiev, in the piano works of his foreign period, relied largely upon techniques developed in his Russian-period works. In his treatment of harmony, however, a certain neo-Classical trend may be perceived in more frequent use of diatonicism in place of chromaticism.

In Prokofiev's piano music of the foreign period, he employs many harmonic techniques that had already become an integral part of his musical language. In the foreign-period works, for example, we find parallelisms, including parallel chords with added tritones in the fifth *Sonata* (third movement, measures 105 and 109) and parallel diminished triads in the "Chose en soi," Opus 45 #1 (Figure 2.58).

Figure 2.58. Prokofiev, "Chose en soi," Opus 45 #1, measures 325-327.
Reprinted by permission of Boosey and Hawkes, Inc.

There are also harmonies based upon unusual scales, such as the mixolydian mode (*Sonata #5*, first movement, opening theme, [Figure 2.59]) and the whole-tone scale (*Sonata #5*, second movement, measures 57-58).

Figure 2.59. Prokofiev, *Sonata #5*, Opus 38, first movement (Allegro tranquillo), measures 1-2. Reprinted by permission of Boosey and Hawkes, Inc.

The influence of *Les Six* and Stravinsky may perhaps be seen in increased use of polychordality and bitonality in the fifth *Sonata* (first movement, measures 76-86; third movement, measures 9-12) and the "Sonatina," Opus 54 #1 (Figure 2.60), although these techniques were already present in Prokofiev's Russian-period piano works.

Figure 2.60. Prokofiev, "Sonatina," Opus 54 #1, first movement (Allegro moderato), measures 162-164. Reprinted by permission of Boosey and Hawkes, Inc.

Rapid modulations to unexpected keys and unusual key relationships still occur frequently (Figure 2.61).

Figure 2.61. Prokofiev, "Sonatina," Opus 54 #2, second movement (Andante amabile), measures 24-25. Reprinted by permission of Boosey and Hawkes, Inc.

Chords with added tones are also common, including such formations as this cluster of minor seconds (Figure 2.62).

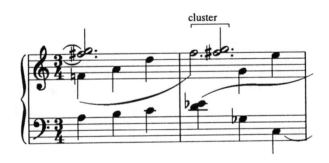

Figure 2.62. Prokofiev, "Chose en soi," Opus 45 #1, measures 305-306. Reprinted by permission of Boosey and Hawkes, Inc.

Harmonic substitution also remains a common device (Figure 2.63).

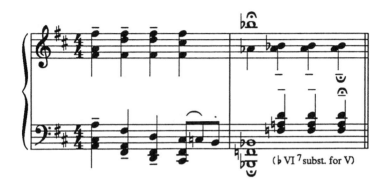

Figure 2.63. Prokofiev, "Pensée," Opus 62 #1, measures 2-3.
Reprinted by permission of Boosey and Hawkes, Inc.

Prokofiev also continued to experiment with ninth, eleventh, and thirteenth chords and with chromatically altered chords (Figure 2.64).

Figure 2.64. Prokofiev, chromatically altered ninth- and eleventh-chords from "Chose en soi," Opus 45 #2, measures 3-4.
Reprinted by permission of Boosey and Hawkes, Inc.

Some harmonic techniques begin to appear in the second period while others disappear. Creation of chords via chromatic motion against pedal points is one technique that disappears. However, as Ashley notes, pedal tones sustained against dissonant harmonies make their debut especially in the *Sonatinas*, Opus 54 #1 (Figure 2.65) and Opus 54 #2 (first movement, second theme).[38]

Figure 2.65. Prokofiev, "Sonatina," Opus 54 #1, first movement (Allegro moderato), measures 9-11. Reprinted by permission of Boosey and Hawkes, Inc.

Quartal chords also appear on occasion but always within a tertian context, as in the fifth *Sonata,* first movement (Figure 2.66); and the "Sonatina," Opus 54 #2, first movement, measure 45.

Figure 2.66. Prokofiev, *Sonata #5,* Opus 38, first movement (Allegro moderato), measure 16. Reprinted by permission of Boosey and Hawkes, Inc.

Also, in the second "Chose en soi," Prokofiev experiments with his own version of impressionistic layering of sonorities (Figure 2.67).

Figure 2.67. Prokofiev, "Chose en soi," Opus 45 #2, measures 26-27. Reprinted by permission of Boosey and Hawkes, Inc.

Finally, we find writing that approaches Schoenbergian atonality in the second "Pensée" (Figure 2.68).

Figure 2.68. Prokofiev, "Pensée," Opus 62 #2, measures 1-3. Reprinted by permission of Boosey and Hawkes, Inc.

Historical context. The years 1918-1935 witnessed the waning of old styles and harmonic techniques and the advent of new ones. A brief overview of harmonic trends in piano music of this period will help to place Prokofiev's foreign-period harmonic practice in its historical context.

In France, *Les Six*, Stravinsky, and Messiaen were all actively composing during this period. Messiaen's book of *Preludes* in 1929 shows the survival of impressionistic harmonic techniques, with the addition of harmonies based upon Messiaen's modes of limited transposition. Milhaud, a member of *Les Six*, explored various polytonal combinations in his *Saudades do Brasil* (1920-1921). Poulenc, another member of *Les Six*, returned to an almost Mozartian diatonicism in several of his piano works, including *Trois mouvements perpetuels* (1918), *Deux novelettes* (1927-1928), and *Huit nocturnes* (1929-1938). Stravinsky, in his *Serenade in A* (1925) also turned toward diatonicism; although, in the first movement of his piano *Sonata* (1924), he employs harmonic substitution and rapid modulation through distant keys.

In Germany and Austria, the most advanced piano music of this period was probably that composed by Hindemith, Krenek, Schoenberg, and Webern. Two devices common to piano music of both Hindemith and Krenek at this time are harmonic substitution and parallelism, seen for example in Hindemith's *Tanzstücke* (1922) and Krenek's *Sonata #2*, Opus 59 (1928). Schoenberg's twelve-tone technique, the most radical compositional innovation of the period, supplies the foundation for such works as Schoenberg's *Suite*, Opus 25 (1921-1923); his *Klavierstücke*, Opus 33 (1928-1931); and Webern's *Variations*, Opus 27 (1935-1936).

In the United States, two trends may be illustrated by works of Copland and Gershwin. Copland experimented with serial techniques in his *Piano Variations* (1930). Jazz influence is found in Gershwin's *Three Preludes* (1926), as well as in several contemporary works by European composers including Stravinsky, Krenek, Milhaud, and Hindemith.

In Russia, Shostakovich's first published works include his *Three Fantastic Dances* for piano, Opus 1. The harmonies in this work rely primarily upon harmonic substitution and side-slipping.

In Hungary, Bartók composed several major piano works during this period including the *Dance Suite* (1925), *Sonata* (1926), and the *Out of Doors* suite (1926). In these works, he utilizes techniques that include parallelism, clusters, and bitonality.

Prokofiev's harmonic practice during the years 1918-1935, although progressive, was not extremely radical. He continued to integrate techniques associated with French impressionism into his style. He used quartal chords sparingly, less radically than Bartók, who had already freely employed parallel quartal chords in his *Bagatelles,* Opus 6 (1908). There are also chord progressions in some of Prokofiev's foreign-period works that sound jazzy (for example, *Sonata #5,* second movement, opening theme); although, as one biographer has remarked, "it remains a question of whether Prokofiev borrowed from jazz or jazz from Prokofiev."[39]

When Prokofiev arrived in Paris in 1920, he was surprised to find that the compositions of the modernists were no more daring than works presented at the Evenings of Modern Music in pre-war St. Petersburg. However, his works written in Paris appear to have been influenced by the prevailing musical taste. His judicious use of diatonicism, harmonic substitution, rapid modulation, and polytonality corresponds to the use of these techniques by his contemporaries, particularly Stravinsky, Milhaud, and Poulenc, who were composing in Paris at that time.

The radical innovations of this period, serialism and the twelve-tone technique, held little appeal for Prokofiev. Despite the fact that he was the first pianist to play Schoenberg in Russia, he did not feel compelled to experiment with Schoenberg's techniques although occasionally his music approaches the border between tonality and atonality.

Melody in Prokofiev's Foreign-period Piano Works

Melodic practice. In the piano works of Prokofiev's foreign period, lyrical melody predominates. Although motivic melody also plays its part, the works of this period show a move away from primitivist repetition of motives. Also, greater emphasis is placed upon diatonic melody in the foreign-period works.

In the works of this period, many of the melodic elements from Prokofiev's first period recur. Melodies are based upon the chromatic scale, various diatonic scales, and the whole-tone scale. Sometimes, Prokofiev combines scale elements in unique ways;

for example, in the second theme of the first movement of the fifth *Sonata,* where he fuses elements of the whole-tone scale and the Phrygian mode (Figure 2.69).[40]

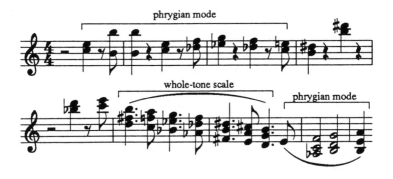

Figure 2.69. Prokofiev, *Sonata #5,* Opus 38, first movement (Allegro tranquillo), measures 26-34. Reprinted by permission of Boosey and Hawkes, Inc.

Octave displacement is still common in the second period (Figure 2.70).

Figure 2.70. Prokofiev, "Sonatina," Opus 54 #1, third movement (Allegretto), measures 21-22. Reprinted by permission of Boosey and Hawkes, Inc.

Melodic substitution remains a trademark (Figure 2.71), but chromatic melodies and counterpoints are less common.

Figure 2.71. Prokofiev, *Sonata #5*, Opus 38, third movement (Un poco allegretto), measure 4. Reprinted by permission of Boosey and Hawkes, Inc.

A new type of melodic pattern that occurs frequently in the second period has been dubbed by Patricia Ashley "the closing-in device."[41] This pattern, shaped like a wedge that narrows to a central point, becomes a salient melodic device especially in the "Sonatina pastorale" (Figure 2.72); in the second subject of this sonatina, "every modulation . . . is effected by a quick closing-in on an unexpected note after a quick one on the expected note".[42]

Figure 2.72. Prokofiev, "Sonatina pastorale," Opus 59 #3, measures 55-56. Reprinted by permission of Boosey and Hawkes, Inc.

Prokofiev probably came closest to creating a twelve-tone tune in the opening of the second "Pensée." Ashley points out that, in this piece, all twelve tones are present in the first twenty-three melody tones, with the third through eleventh tones all different (Figure 2.73).[43]

Figure 2.73. Prokofiev, "Pensée," Opus 62 #2, measures 1-7.
Reprinted by permission of Boosey and Hawkes, Inc.

Historical context. A survey of melodic techniques during the years 1918-1935 will help to clarify the historical position of Prokofiev as a melodist in his foreign-period piano works.

In France, in Messiaen's *Preludes* (1929), impressionistic melodic techniques still thrived, enriched by the addition of melodies based upon modes of limited transposition. Also in France, the influence of neo-Classicism may be seen in the diatonic melodies of Poulenc's early works. The influence of neo-Baroque aesthetics may also be seen in the modified Bachian melodies and ornamentation of the second and third movements of Stravinsky's *Sonata* (1924).

In Germany and Austria in the 1920's, Hindemith and Krenek were influenced by jazz. Their melodies also employ side-slipping and octave displacement. In the same decade in Vienna, Schoenberg was experimenting with twelve-tone melody. His student, Webern, would eventually introduce pointillistic twelve-tone melody into piano literature in his *Variations* (1935-1936).

Works by composers in other countries show both the commonality and diversity of melodic practice during this period. In the United States, serialist motivic technique was a strong factor in Copland's *Piano Variations*, while American jazz influenced such works as Gershwin's *Three Preludes* (1926). In Russia, Shostakovich's *Three Fantastic Dances* (1922) utilized side-slipping and octave displacement. In Hungary, Bartók introduced into his works of the period melodies based upon Eastern European folk materials as well as such melodic techniques as substitution and octave displacement. Prokofiev's melodic practice during the period 1918-1935 was neither revolutionary nor exceptionally conservative. In melody, as in harmony, he continued to incorporate techniques associated with impressionism into his music. In his use of diatonic melody, melodic side-slipping, and octave displacement, he kept pace with many of his European contemporaries. However, he avoided or scorned many contemporary developments. He openly criticized Stravinsky's neo-Bachisms. He also cared little for serialist, twelve-tone, and pointillistic melodic experiments, although he may have given a passing nod to Schoenberg in the opening melody of his second "Pensée."

Rhythm and Meter in Prokofiev's Foreign-period Piano Works

Rhythmic practice. In the foreign-period works, Prokofiev moved away from the aggressive, motoric rhythmic drive that characterized several of his early piano works. Even when motoric rhythms appear, as in portions of the fifth *Sonata,* the tempos tend to be moderate or slow.

In the foreign-period works, he rarely used polyrhythms and polymeter. However, he did introduce metric changes within a movement more frequently than in the first period.

Historical context. The historical context of Prokofiev's rhythmic practice during the years 1918-1935 will be clarified by a brief survey of rhythmic practices in the music of his contemporaries during the same period.

Certain rhythmic elements were integrated into the mainstream of art music during this period. Jazz syncopation, one of the pervasive rhythmic elements of the early twentieth century, appears in such diverse works as Gershwin's *Three Preludes,* Stravinsky's *Piano-rag-music* (1919), and Hindemith's *Suite 1922.* Another development, one that gained momentum after Stravinsky's *Rite of Spring,* was the technique of frequently changing meter (multimeter), seen in such works as Bartók's piano *Sonata* (1926).

Some composers of the period experimented with rather idiosyncratic rhythmic techniques. Stravinsky's *Piano-rag-music* (1919), like portions of Ives's *"Concord" Sonata,* dispensed with regular bar lines. Messiaen, in certain of his preludes, introduced metric changes that are based upon added values of a sixteenth note within the measure. The Brazilian composer Heitor Villa-Lobos used patterns from folk music that are similar to additive rhythms in his *Prole do Bébé* No. 3 ("The Clay Doll"), written in 1918. Schoenberg's innovative rhythms tend to consist of alternating groups of shorter and longer note-values, while Webern in his *Variations,* Opus 27, employed silence in innovative ways.

Rhythmically, Prokofiev was rather conservative in the piano works of his foreign period. Aside from the more frequent appearance of metric changes within a movement, we find little innovation and an almost total neglect of the most striking rhythmic devices of his early piano works.

Prokofiev's move away from expressionism toward a reserved neo-Classicism helps to account for the more sedate, conventional rhythms of his foreign period. His rhythms during this period show greater similarity to the rhythms found in other neo-Classical works than to the rhythms of more radical or expressionistic contemporary works.

Texture in Prokofiev's Foreign-period Piano Works

Textural practice. In these works, Prokofiev's textures range from strictly homophonic to contrapuntal. As in the first period, chord progressions often appear to be determined by voice-leading rather than function (Figure 2.74).

Figure 2.74. Prokofiev, *Sonata #5,* Opus 38, second movement (Andantino), measures 9-13. Reprinted by permission of Boosey and Hawkes, Inc.

Compared with the works of the first period, however, there is a significant scarcity of Alberti-bass or broken-chord accompaniments, a notable exception being the opening theme of the third movement of the fifth *Sonata.* Ostinato is also rare in the second-period works.

Freedom of voice-leading permeates much of the music of the second period. Solo melodic lines that are unaccompanied, as well as those doubled at the octave or fifteenth, play a significant role in the first movement of the fifth *Sonata.* As Ashley observes, one device, featured more frequently in the second period, is the use of parallel octaves between soprano and bass, in order to draw attention to certain notes or motives within a theme (e.g., *Sonata #5*, Opus 38, first movement, measures 2-3; and "Promenade," Opus 59 #1, measure 4).[44] Another new device is a kind of neo-impressionistic layering found in the second "Chose en soi" (Figure 2.75).

Figure 2.75. Prokofiev, "Chose en soi," Opus 45 #2, measures 77-78.
Reprinted by permission of Boosey and Hawkes, Inc.

Two-voice counterpoint makes its appearance more frequently in the second period (e.g., "Chose en soi," Opus 45 #2, measures 1-2; "Sonatina," Opus 54 #1, second movement, measures 1-2). A related textural innovation consists of expansion of two-part counterpoint into additional voices by doubling at the fifteenth (Figure 2.76).

Figure 2.76. Prokofiev, "Pensée," Opus 62 #1, measures 11-13.
Reprinted by permission of Boosey and Hawkes, Inc.

Historical context. In order to place Prokofiev's choice of textures in the foreign period into historical context, let us begin with a brief overview of textural practice in piano works by his contemporaries during the years 1918-1935.

Homophony is present in various piano works of the period, including several of Poulenc's early works, Krenek's second *Sonata*, Hindemith's *Suite 1922*, and Shostakovich's *Three Fantastic Dances*. Accompaniment figures found in this period include the Alberti-bass patterns of Poulenc's "Mouvements perpetuels" and the ostinatos of Bartók's *Sonata, Improvisations*, and *Out of Doors*.

The rise of neo-Classicism brought increased emphasis upon counterpoint. The third movement of Stravinsky's *Sonata*, for example, begins with a neo-Bachian fugato. The second movement of Webern's *Variations* is comprised of a series of canons in inversion. Dissonant counterpoint ranging from two to five voices characterizes much of Schoenberg's *Suite*, Opus 25 (1925). Webern bases the first movement of his variations upon a counterpoint of overlapping twelve-tone motives.

Some far-reaching textural experiments took place during the period 1918-1935. The "Night Music" from Bartók's *Out of Doors* consists largely of isolated motives that suggest the random noises of nocturnal insects. In the Webern *Variations*, the texture of the third movement could be considered "a counterpoint of sound and silence."[45]

Prokofiev's exploration of textures in the piano music of his foreign period was conservative. Although his foreign-period works occasionally feature dissonant counterpoint, the textures are hardly ever academically contrapuntal or unusually complex. Also, since Prokofiev remained primarily a thematic composer, he avoided the trend toward dissolution of line foreshadowed by Bartók and Webern.

Form in Prokofiev's Foreign-Period Piano Works

Formal practice. In the piano works of his foreign period, Prokofiev utilized traditional and original forms. He continued to rely primarily upon sonata form, ternary (ABA) form, and various rondo forms. Within the sonata form, however, we are more likely to find unusual key relationships. The "Sonatina pastorale" in C, for example, modulates to B-flat for its second subject and to other keys within the whole-tone scale of C during the development. Prokofiev also experimented for the first time with fantasia-like through-composed works comprised of sections with different key- and time-signatures (e.g., *Choses en soi,* Opus 45; "Promenade," Opus 59 #1). Generally in the piano works from Opus 45 to Opus 62, we also encounter irregular phrasing and overlapping phrases more frequently than before.

Historical context. A brief overview of forms and formal techniques in contemporary piano works from 1918 to 1935 will help to place Prokofiev's formal practice during this period into historical perspective.

The three- or four-movement sonata, having a first movement in sonata form, was one of the forms favored during the years 1918-1935 by Prokofiev's contemporaries. Stravinsky, Bartók, and Krenek all contributed to this genre during these years.

The suite was another favored genre, of which Bartók's *Out of Doors,* Hindemith's *Suite 1922,* and Schoenberg's *Suite,* Opus 25, provide outstanding examples. Other contemporary collections of pieces such as Milhaud's *Saudades do Brasil* could possibly also be considered suites.

Revival and modernization of Baroque forms and formal techniques played an important role during this period. Besides the dance suite, we encounter, for example, a *Toccata and Chaconne* by Krenek and a fugato in Stravinsky's *Sonata*.

In the 1920's, variation form underwent a radical redefinition with the advent of serialism and the twelve-tone technique. Even Schoenberg's most through-composed twelve-tone works could be considered variations on a tone-row.

In the more forward-looking piano works of this period, irregular phrasing is fairly common. Regular phrasing tends to appear in works based upon dance forms, such as Hindemith's *Suite 1922*.

Prokofiev's formal practice during his foreign period proves to be somewhat conservative. His preference for well-established forms has its counterpart in the preferences of many of his contemporaries during the same period. His experimentation with fantasia-like structures could perhaps be considered innovative. However, in his foreign-period works, he avoids neo-Baroque forms and techniques as well as the radical formal innovations associated with serialism and the twelve-tone technique.

Pianistic Technique in Prokofiev's Foreign-period Piano Works

Practice. Prokofiev's foreign-period piano works show a turn away from extroverted bravura display. We find no Prokofiev etudes or toccatas in this period, nor do we find movements in extremely fast tempi. While there are a few crossed-hand passages, the kind of rapid hand-crossing encountered in several works from the first period virtually disappears. Technical difficulties tend to arise instead from complexities of texture that require rapid changes of hand position, rather than from virtuosic writing. Also, very few passages in the piano music of this period call for a percussive staccato touch.

Historical context. During Prokofiev's foreign period, several composers were strongly influenced by neo-Classical restraint in their approach to pianism. Romantic glorification of virtuosity took second place to musical construction, in a trend that may be illustrated by comparing Stravinsky's neo-Classical *Serenade* (1925) and *Sonata* (1924) with two of Stravinsky's earlier works, the *Four Etudes* (1907) and the *Three Movements from Petrouchka* (1921).

Notable exceptions to this anti-virtuosic trend occur, however. For example, in the first and second movements of Webern's *Variations*, Opus 27, the composer deliberately divides the material between the hands to provide for the maximum amount of leaping and hand-crossing. During this same period, certain piano works of Henry Cowell re-define the phrase "playing the piano"; they call for such non-traditional performance techniques as plucking and strumming the strings.

The restraint evident in Prokofiev's approach to pianistic technique in his foreign period could be considered a product of the neo-Classical trend in the arts and therefore historically in step with that movement. That same period, however, continued to see the production of virtuosic works by several of Prokofiev's contemporaries, as well as the development of some radically new playing techniques which Prokofiev did not see fit to adopt.

The Soviet Period (1936-1953)

Biographical Notes

Prokofiev returned to the land of his birth in 1936 and chose to remain there for the rest of his life. Prokofiev enjoyed for many years the status of a national hero in the Soviet Union, receiving many state honors for his work. He was also able to work comfortably in one of the colonies for Soviet composers during the Second World War and was occasionally allowed to travel abroad. During a visit to the Disney studios and other Hollywood studios, he learned the ropes of cinematic production, gaining knowledge that served him well in his collaboration with Soviet filmmaker Sergei Eisenstein. Several of Prokofiev's greatest and most successful works were composed during the Soviet period, including *Peter and the Wolf*, the ballet *Cinderella*, the opera *War and Peace*, and the late piano sonatas.

It is sad that, although Prokofiev enjoyed many fruitful years of popularity in his homeland, as a Soviet composer he had to live with the constant threat of bureaucratic condemnation that hovered over Soviet artists. Shortly after his arrival, he learned of the official denunciation, by the Soviet news publication *Pravda*, of Shostakovich's opera *Lady Macbeth of Mtensk*. In later years, he had to endure the disappearance of his close associate, the theatrical director Vsevolod Meyerhold; the periodic denunciation of his own music; and the sentencing of his estranged first wife, Lina Llubera,[46] to eight years in a Siberian labor camp.

In 1945, Prokofiev fell down a flight of stairs and suffered a severe concussion. He continued to compose, as much as his health permitted, for the remaining years of his life. His death occurred on March 5, 1953, the same day as the death of Stalin.

Style in Prokofiev's Soviet-period Piano Works

The piano music of Prokofiev's Soviet period includes the following works:

Opus 82, *Sonata #6,* A minor, 1939-1940
Opus 83, *Sonata #7,* B-flat, 1939-1942
Opus 84, *Sonata #8,* B-flat, 1939-1944
Opus 103, *Sonata #9,* C major, 1947

Prokofiev's Soviet-period works also include a significant number of transcriptions for piano of excerpts from his ballet, opera, and film scores. This chapter will focus upon style in the Soviet-period sonatas, however, since they were written solely for piano. A discussion of the transcriptions will be saved for a later chapter that will focus upon their pedagogical value.

In the Soviet-period piano sonatas, Prokofiev returned to aesthetics and techniques established in his first period. In the sixth, seventh, and eighth *Sonatas*—three monumental works composed during the Second World War—we find a resurgence of neo-Romantic and expressionist aesthetics. In the ninth *Sonata,* written in 1947, Prokofiev simplifies the textures and harmonies considerably but still utilizes essentially the same techniques.

Harmony in Prokofiev's Soviet-period Piano Works

Harmonic practice. Harmonically, Prokofiev's Soviet-period piano works, even at their most complex, rely largely upon techniques developed in the piano works of his first period. We find examples of:

a)   side-slipping and substitution;

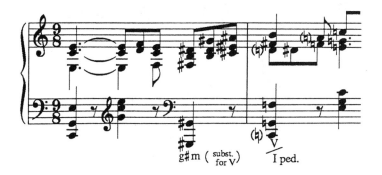

Figure 2.77. Prokofiev, *Sonata #6*, Opus 82, third movement
(Tempo di valser lentissimo), measures 1-2. Used with the permission of G. Schirmer, Inc.,
New York (ASCAP) on behalf of RAIS (Russia).

Figure 2.78. Prokofiev, *Sonata #6*, Opus 82, first movement
(Allegro moderato), measure 6. Used with the permission of G. Schirmer, Inc.,
New York (ASCAP) on behalf of RAIS (Russia).

b) creation of new chords by chromatic motion against pedal points;

Figures 2.79, 2.80. Prokofiev, *Sonata #7*, Opus 83, third movement (Precipitato), measures 11-13; and *Sonata #6*, Opus 82, second movement (Allegretto), measure 14. Used with the permission of G. Schirmer, Inc., New York (ASCAP) on behalf of RAIS (Russia).

c) harmonic elision;

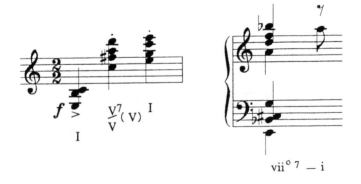

Figures 2.81, 2.82. Prokofiev, *Sonata #6*, Opus 82, second movement (Allegretto), measure 36; and *Sonata #7*, Opus 83, first movement (Allegro inquieto), measure 178. Used with the permission of G. Schirmer, Inc., New York (ASCAP) on behalf of RAIS (Russia).

d) parallelism;

Figure 2.83. Prokofiev, *Sonata #8*, Opus 84, second movement (Andante sognando), measure 47. Used with the permission of G. Schirmer, Inc., New York (ASCAP) on behalf of RAIS (Russia).

e) harmonies based upon unusual scales;

(whole-tone scale in bass)

Figure 2.84. Prokofiev, *Sonata #9*, Opus 103, fourth movement (Allegro con brio, ma non troppo presto), measures 27-29. Used with the permission of G. Schirmer, Inc., New York (ASCAP) on behalf of RAIS (Russia).

f) unexpected modulations to foreign keys and unusual key relationships;

Figure 2.85. Prokofiev, *Sonata #6*, Opus 82, second movement (Allegretto), measures 91-92. Used with the permission of G. Schirmer, Inc., New York (ASCAP) on behalf of RAIS (Russia).

Figure 2.86. Prokofiev, *Sonata #7*, Opus 83, second movement (Andante caloroso), measures 22-24. Used with the permission of G. Schirmer, Inc., New York (ASCAP) on behalf of RAIS (Russia).

g) chromatic harmonies and chromaticism;

Figure 2.87. Prokofiev, *Sonata #6*, Opus 82, third movement (Tempo di valser lentissimo), measure 50. Used with the permission of G. Schirmer, Inc., New York (ASCAP) on behalf of RAIS (Russia).

Figure 2.88. Prokofiev, *Sonata #7*, Opus 83, second movement (Andante caloroso), measures 44-45. Used with the permission of G. Schirmer, Inc., New York (ASCAP) on behalf of RAIS (Russia).

h) polychords and bitonality;

Figure 2.89. Prokofiev, *Sonata #7*, Opus 83, first movement (Allegro inquieto), measures 260-261. Used with the permission of G. Schirmer, Inc., New York (ASCAP) on behalf of RAIS (Russia).

Figure 2.90. Prokofiev, *Sonata #6*, Opus 82, second movement (Allegretto), measures 30-32. Used with the permission of G. Schirmer, Inc., New York (ASCAP) on behalf of RAIS (Russia).

and i) chords with added tones.

Figures 2.91, 2.92, 2.93. Prokofiev, *Sonata #6,* Opus 82, first movement
(Allegro moderato), measures 1 and 39; *Sonata #7,* Opus 83, first movement
(Allegro inquieto), measure 45. Used with the permission of G. Schirmer, Inc.,
New York (ASCAP) on behalf of RAIS (Russia).

Examples of these techniques, with the exception of harmonic elision
and harmonies based upon unusual scales, are abundant in both the
late sonatas and the early works.

   Historical Context. The years 1936-1953 saw the advent of
theoretical, pedagogical, and concert works representing a wide variety
of styles and harmonic practices. In 1937-1939, Hindemith published
the two volumes of his *Craft of Musical Composition,* in which he
attempted to codify a system of tonal harmony containing harmonic
classifications broad enough to include sonorities typical of twentieth-
century music.   In 1939, Bartók completed the *Mikrokosmos,* a
pedagogical work containing 153 pieces in all, designed to introduce
the student to many of the techniques and materials of twentieth-
century music. Harmonically, this work affords examples of modality,
bitonality, chromatic motion against pedal points, added tritones,
clusters, and sonorities built from minor seconds, major sevenths, and

perfect fourths and fifths. During the same period, Messiaen's *Vingt regards sur l'Enfant-Jésus* (1944) continues the harmonic legacy of impressionism, while jazz harmonies color Copland's *Four Piano Blues* (1926-1948), and serialism dictates the harmonies of Krenek's fourth *Sonata* (1948) and Messiaen's "Modes de valeurs et d'intensités" (1951).

Prokofiev's harmonic practice during the Soviet period shows marked conservatism, a preference for consolidation rather than innovation.   While many composers were experimenting with serialism and the twelve-tone technique, Prokofiev and other Soviet composers avoided these techniques, either from personal conviction or from fear of state persecution.

By this time, many of the daring techniques of Prokofiev's youth had become part of the common language of contemporary music. His practice of harmonic substitution fits quite respectably into Hindemith's system of chordal classification.   His use of modality, bitonality, and chords with added tones continued to give his harmony a twentieth-century stamp, even though he was less adventurous in his later years than Bartók, Messiaen, and many other composers.

Melody in Prokofiev's Soviet-period Piano Works

Melodic practice. Melodically, Prokofiev also relies in his Soviet-period piano works upon techniques developed in his first period. It is not difficult to find examples of:

a)   the amusing Prokofiev tune;

Figure 2.94. Prokofiev, *Sonata #8*, Opus 84, third movement (Vivace), measures 42-45.
Used with the permission of G. Schirmer, Inc., New York (ASCAP)
on behalf of RAIS (Russia).

b)   the angular serious melody;

Figure 2.95. Prokofiev, *Sonata #7,* Opus 83, first movement (Allegro inquieto),
measures 126-130. Used with the permission of G. Schirmer, Inc., New York (ASCAP)
on behalf of RAIS (Russia).

c)   melodies based upon unusual or chromatically altered
scales;

Figure 2.96. Prokofiev, *Sonata #8,* Opus 84, first movement (Andante dolce),
measures 61-62. Used with the permission of G. Schirmer, Inc., New York (ASCAP)
on behalf of RAIS (Russia).

Figure 2.97. Prokofiev, *Sonata #6*, Opus 82, fourth movement (Vivace), measures 1-2.
Used with the permission of G. Schirmer, Inc., New York (ASCAP)
on behalf of RAIS (Russia).

and d) motivic melodies.

Figure 2.98 a and b. Prokofiev, *Sonata #7*, Opus 83., third movement (Precipitato),
measures 1-2 and measures 52-54. Used with the permission of G. Schirmer, Inc.,
New York (ASCAP) on behalf of RAIS (Russia).

In the late sonatas, Prokofiev sometimes included melodies that are reminiscent of sentimental popular tunes. Three outstanding examples of such melodies are the opening themes of the slow movements of the sixth, seventh, and eighth *Sonatas*.

Figure 2.99. Prokofiev, *Sonata #7*, Opus 83, second movement (Andante caloroso), measures 1-3. Used with the permission of G. Schirmer, Inc., New York (ASCAP) on behalf of RAIS (Russia).

Historical context. The period from 1936-1953 witnessed a diversity of melodic practice among contemporary composers. In Bartók's *Mikrokosmos,* completed in 1939, we find melodies derived from a cornucopia of scales: church modes; Oriental, Arabic, Balinese, and jazz scales; pentatonic and whole-tone scales; plus a few scales of Bartók's own invention. In Messiaen's works of this period, we find melodies derived from birdsong and from various scales including modes of limited transposition. Melodic substitution is found in Hindemith's *Ludus Tonalis,* while the twelve-tone technique provides the melodic material for such works as Krenek's fourth *Sonata.* Cage's pieces for prepared piano during the 1940's introduced a new factor into melodic writing for piano, that of alteration of timbre.

Prokofiev's melodic practice during the Soviet period was neither adventuresome nor entirely conservative. He continued to reject serialism. He never explored the melodic resources of the prepared piano. He did, however, derive melodies from modal and whole-tone scales and occasionally invented scales through chromatic alteration of modes. He also continued to exploit melodic substitution and octave displacement and to approach melodic atonality on occasion.

Rhythm and Meter in Prokofiev's Soviet-period Piano Works

Rhythmic practice.   In   the   Soviet-period   piano   works,
rhythmic techniques developed in Prokofiev's early period appear in
key places.   The principle of perpetual motion or motoric rhythm,
together with the choice of an asymmetrical meter (7/8), makes the
toccata finale of the seventh *Sonata* one of the great *tours de force* of
twentieth-century piano literature.   Ostinatos, *stile mécanique* figures,
and offbeat rhythms also contribute to the relentless dynamism of this
toccata finale (Figure 2.100).

Figure 2.100.   Ostinato figures and offbeat rhythms in Prokofiev's *Sonata #7*,
third movement (Precipitato), measures 15-16 and 57-58.   Used with the permission of
G. Schirmer, Inc., New York (ASCAP) on behalf of RAIS (Russia).

Polymeter (6/8 against 3/4) makes a brief appearance in the first
movement of the seventh *Sonata* (Figure 2.101), although polyrhythm
and polymeter are very rare in Prokofiev's Soviet-period sonatas.

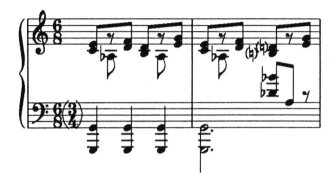

Figure 2.101. Polymeter in Prokofiev's *Sonata #7*, first movement (Allegro inquieto), measures 265-266. Used with the permission of G. Schirmer, Inc., New York (ASCAP) on behalf of RAIS (Russia).

In the sixth *Sonata*, Prokofiev introduces some ragtime syncopation. Otherwise, he draws upon the same rhythmic vocabulary in his late sonatas as he does in his early works.

Historical context. During Prokofiev's Soviet period (1936-1953), composers elaborated upon established rhythmic techniques and invented new ones. Bartók's *Mikrokosmos* offers the pianist a compendium of established rhythmic techniques including rapidly changing meters, additive meter, polyrhythms, non-coinciding meters, and, according to Benjamin Suchoff, six hundred thirty-six different patterns of syncopation.[47]

Among new developments, Messiaen's rhythmic experiments should be mentioned. In his works of this period, he draws upon a personal rhythmic vocabulary that includes non-retrogradable (palindrome) rhythms, Hindu rhythms, non-integral augmentations and diminutions, rhythms derived from birdsong, and rhythms with added values. Messiaen also provides us with one of the first examples of rhythmic serialization in his "Modes de valeurs et d'intensités" from the *Quatre etudes de rhythme;* this technique was taken to an extreme of complexity in Stockhausen's *Klavierstücke I-IV* (1952-1953).

Among experiments in American piano music, Elliott Carter's technique of metric modulation, found in his *Sonata* (1945-1946), deserves mention. This term refers to gradual changes of meter through equivalencies of note-values and tempos.

Prokofiev's rhythmic practice in the Soviet-period sonatas again illustrates a trend toward conservatism in his later years. He preferred to consolidate time-tested rhythmic techniques rather than to experiment or to borrow other composers' innovations. Despite the fact that Prokofiev no longer kept pace with the avant-garde, the finales of the late sonatas nonetheless show that he had not lost his youthful vitality.

Texture in Prokofiev's Soviet-period Piano Works

Textural practice. Since the solo piano works of Prokofiev's first two periods display a variety of textures, it should not be surprising to see many of these textures recur in his later works. The Soviet-period sonatas, like the earlier works, contain examples of chordal writing, broken-chord accompaniments, dissonant counterpoint, academic contrapuntal techniques, and textures that combine elements of both homophony and counterpoint; (for example, combination of a melody in the soprano, a harmonically governed bass line, and subordinate counterpoint in a middle voice or voices). In his late piano sonatas, Prokofiev tends to change textures more frequently and with greater subtlety than in his early works, treating voice-leading with the freedom found in many of his foreign-period works (Figure 2.102).

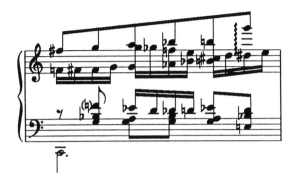

Figure 2.102. Prokofiev, *Sonata #7*, Opus 83, second movement (Andante caloroso), measures 48-50. Used with the permission of G. Schirmer, Inc., New York (ASCAP) on behalf of RAIS (Russia).

Historical context. During Prokofiev's Soviet period, contemporary composers made use of a great variety of textures. If we turn again to Bartók's *Mikrokosmos*, we find examples of textures ranging from pure homophony to academic counterpoint. A list of textural techniques from this work alone would include solid- and broken-chord accompaniments, chordal stretto, ostinato, imitation, stretto, inversion, strict and free canon, two-part invention style, mirroring, and buzzing effects produced by contrapuntal clashes of minor seconds against sustained tones. In this same period, fugal technique was revived, especially by Hindemith and Shostakovich. Pointillistic texture was continued in works by Stockhausen and Messiaen. Arguably, the most far-reaching textural development, however, was Cage's invention of the prepared piano, since it extended the range of possible piano textures by adding a new vocabulary of percussive sounds.

Prokofiev's Soviet-period sonatas offer examples of many textures present in other notable contemporary piano compositions. However, Prokofiev never introduced neo-Baroque contrapuntal techniques into his piano works, nor did he explore pointillistic textures or unusual effects such as harmonics, buzzing, reaching inside the piano, or piano preparation.

Form in Prokofiev's Soviet-period Piano Works

Formal practice.   Prokofiev's treatment of form in the Soviet-period sonatas is similar to his treatment of form in his Russian-period piano works.   He chooses sonata, ternary (ABA), and rondo forms, just as he did in his early works.   Also, the last four sonatas, like the second *Sonata*, exhibit elements of cyclic form.
In the late sonatas, two developments should be noted.   One is an expansion of formal dimensions, evident in the outer movements of the sixth, seventh, and eighth *Sonatas.*   The other is the elaborate and original cyclic scheme of the ninth *Sonata:*   in each of the first three movements of this sonata, the coda introduces the principal theme of the movement to come, while the coda of the fourth movement quotes the opening theme of the first movement.
The greater sophistication of many of Prokofiev's later sonatas, as compared with the earlier ones, is seen in subtleties of structure.   Asymmetrical and overlapping phrases are much more common in the later sonatas than in the earlier ones.   Sequences are less common in the later sonatas, but variation of motives, with or without extensions, is more common.

Historical context.   While Prokofiev's output of works for piano during the years 1936-1953 was restricted to sonatas and transcriptions from other media, his contemporaries were at work in several genres, composing sonatas, preludes and fugues, piano cycles, and collections of shorter works for piano.   During this period, Elliott Carter, Samuel Barber, Leon Kirchner, and Ernst Krenek number among the composers who made important contributions to the literature of the piano sonata.   Two collections of preludes and fugues written during this period—Hindemith's *Ludus Tonalis* and Shostakovich's *Twenty-four Preludes and Fugues*—continue the neo-Baroque trend in paying homage to Bach's *Well-Tempered Clavier.*   Among the piano cycles and collections of short pieces, outstanding contributions were made by Messiaen in his *Vingt regards sur l'Enfant-Jésus* and by Bartók in his *Mikrokosmos.*
Prokofiev chose in his Soviet-period years to expand the sonata form and to experiment further with cyclic form.   In these respects, his late sonatas share characteristics with Beethoven's later sonatas and sonatas by the nineteenth-centry Romantics.   Prokofiev's

commitment to tradition, however, never extended to the revival of Baroque genres, such as the prelude and fugue, even though these genres attracted several of his contemporaries.

Pianistic Technique in Prokofiev's Soviet-period Piano Works

Practice. Technically, Prokofiev's Soviet-period sonatas, like the sonatas of his first period, contain many formidable virtuoso passages. While rapid hand-crossing does not return to favor in the later sonatas, arpeggios, glissandi, and scales reappear in key places. Rapid leaps appear especially in the first movement of the sixth *Sonata* and the first movement and finale of the seventh *Sonata*. In passages involving rapid leaps from chord to chord, the difficulty is often compounded in the later sonatas by awkward changes of hand position (Figure 2.103).

Figure 2.103. Prokofiev, *Sonata #7*, Opus 83, third movement (Precipitato), measures 152-153. Used with the permission of G. Schirmer, Inc., New York (ASCAP) on behalf of RAIS (Russia).

Tone clusters in Prokofiev's piano music appear for the first and last time in the sixth *Sonata*, where they are marked "col pugno" (with the fist).

Figure 2.104. Prokofiev, *Sonata #6*, Opus 82, first movement (Allegro moderato), measure 141. Used with the permission of G. Schirmer, Inc., New York (ASCAP) on behalf of RAIS (Russia).

Historical context. During the years 1936-1953, composers tended to go their separate ways in their treatment of pianistic technique. Shostakovich and Hindemith each wrote collections of preludes and fugues, exploiting those technical difficulties inherent in contrapuntal playing. Difficulties associated with rhythmic complexity and rapid leaps characterize Messiaen's *Quatre etudes de rhythme* and Stockhausen's *Klavierstücke I-IV*. The Carter *Sonata* creates some striking effects through pianistic harmonics. Although Bartók wrote no virtuosic pieces during this period, his *Mikrokosmos* offers a pedagogical method that is particularly valuable for developing independence of the hands and fingers and for the introduction of twentieth-century idioms.

During his years as a Soviet composer, Prokofiev contributed more than any of his contemporaries to the standard repetoire of the piano sonata. His "War" sonatas, all admirably pianistic, upheld many established virtuoso techniques with a vigor that has helped to ensure the lasting place of these works in the virtuoso repertory.

Chapter III

A PEDAGOGICAL INTRODUCTION TO THE
PIANO WORKS OF PROKOFIEV

From a pedagogical viewpoint, Prokofiev's piano works may be conveniently divided into four categories:

A. Works written for pedagogical use
B. Advanced-intermediate-level works
C. Advanced-level or concert works
D. Transcriptions

In this chapter, those works that fall under each of these category headings will be discussed individually. A thumbnail description of each piece will be given and a few words said specifically about that particular piece's technical challenges, aesthetic value, and suitability for teaching or performance. Remarks as to the quality of a piece of music must invariably remain subjective, however well-founded they may be. Any such remarks made in this chapter are meant merely to guide the teacher or student toward what are probably the most interesting and rewarding piano works of Prokofiev; they are not intended as a substitute for first-hand acquaintance with the music itself.

Works Written for Pedagogical Use

Music for Children, Opus 65

Of those pieces written specifically with pedagogical intent, only one group of pieces is clearly designed to appeal to young students: Prokofiev's *Music for Children*, Opus 65. However, the title *Music for Children* should not dissuade adults from studying and enjoying these pieces, especially since their subtleties of musical content and technique may, in many instances, be better appreciated by adults.

This opus contains twelve pieces, each prefaced by a title easily understood by young students (with one possible exception being the title "Tarantella," which may require a few words of explanation by the teacher). The twelve titles in Opus 65 are:

    1) "Morning"
    2) "Walk"
    3) "Fairy Tale"
    4) "Tarantella"
    5) "Regrets"
    6) "Waltz"
    7) "Parade of the Grasshoppers"
    8) "The Rain and the Rainbow"
    9) "Tag"
   10) "March"
   11) "Evening"
   12) "Moonlit Meadow"

These twelve pieces may be performed individually, but they also lend themselves to performance as a cycle, beginning appropriately enough with "Morning" and ending with "Evening" and "Moonlit Meadow." Prokofiev himself orchestrated seven of these pieces (Opus 65 #1, 9, 6, 5, 10, 11, and 12) to create the *Summer Day* suite, Opus 65b.

The first piece of Opus 65, "Morning" (Figure 3.1), is based upon familiar scale patterns and triads in the key of C. It features hand-crossing, leaps, contrasts of register, and two-note slurs ascending and descending.

Andante tranquillo

Figure 3.1. Prokofiev, "Morning," Opus 65 #1, measures 1-3.
Figures 3.1. through 3.12., from Opus 65, are reprinted
by permission of Boosey and Hawkes, Inc.

The second piece of Opus 65, "Walk" (Figure 3.2), begins in C Major, but modulates to G and E-flat in the course of its development. This piece also contains some easy crossed-hand passages. Additionally, this piece may be used to teach left-hand triplets.

Figure 3.2. Prokofiev, "Walk," Opus 65 #2, measures 1-5.

"Fairy Tale," Opus 65 #3 (Figure 3.3), carries the marking "Adagio," and requires the extra measure of sensitive control associated with very slow playing. It could be used to teach the rhythm ♫♩ that occurs throughout.

Figure 3.3. Prokofiev, "Fairy Tale," Opus 65 #3, measures 1-3.

The "Tarantella," Opus 65 #4 (Figure 3.4), may be used to introduce the tarantella to lower-intermediate students. The teacher may wish to spark the student's interest by offering the traditional explanation of the tarantella as an Italian dance originally created to ward off the effects of the tarantula's bite. The teacher may also want to describe the actions associated with the dance, especially skipping, running, and banging of tambourines, in order to give the student a feeling for the lively 6/8 rhythms of this dance. Technically, in this piece, fast broken triads and five-finger patterns dominate. Musically, rapid key changes abound; for example, the transitions from D minor to D-flat major and then A-flat major within the first nine measures.

Figure 3.4. Prokofiev, "Tarantella," Opus 65 #4, measures 1-4.

The fifth piece of Opus 65, "Regrets" (Figure 3.5), evokes a deeply sorrowful mood, as its title suggests. It employs broken chords and scale melodies, and requires some contrapuntal division of the right hand between melody and accompaniment.

Figure 3.5. Prokofiev, "Regrets," Opus 65 #5, measures 1-4.

The sixth piece, "Waltz," Opus 65 #6 (Figure 3.6), could be used to introduce jump-bass patterns to a student at the lower-intermediate level. The melody of the "A" section should be performed smoothly, despite the octave displacements so characteristic of Prokofiev. The "B" section calls for confident hand-crossing and changes of register.

Figure 3.6. Prokofiev, "Waltz, Opus 65 #6, measures 1-4.

"Parade of the Grasshoppers," the seventh piece of Opus 65 (Figure 3.7), well deserves its catchy title. It begins with a jaunty march in 2/4 that contains many humorous far-flung leaps. The more lyrical middle section modulates to E-flat and B; this section may help to encourage an intermediate student to read in these somewhat complex and intimidating keys.

Figure 3.7. Prokofiev, "Parade of the Grasshoppers," Opus 65 #7, measures 1-4.

"The Rain and the Rainbow," Opus 65 #8 (Figure 3.8), has an appealing and easily explained programmatic title. Those sections associated with the rain make use of rapid crescendi and diminuendi, black- and white-key clusters of seconds, and a widely spaced bass pattern. These contrast with the dolce melodies of the rainbow sections.

Figure 3.8. Prokofiev, "The Rain and the Rainbow," Opus 65 #8, measures 1-2.

"Tag," Opus 65 #9 (Figure 3.9), readily conjures up images of a familiar children's game. The lively 6/8 perpetual-motion passage work vividly suggests running and chasing. The division of melodic lines between the hands could even be connected with the idea of first one hand and then the other being "tagged."

Figure 3.9. Prokofiev, "Tag," Opus 65 #9, measures 1-4.

In the "March," Opus 65 #10 (Figure 3.10), Prokofiev has given us a technically easy introduction to his sassy, ironic march style. The harmonic techniques employed in this piece include clusters and added tones.

Figure 3.10. Prokofiev, "March," Opus 65 #10, measures 3-4.

"Evening," Opus 65 #11 (Figure 3.11), is a tranquil, lyrical mood-piece. Its broken-chord figures could be used to teach rotary movements.

Figure 3.11. Prokofiev, "Evening," Opus 65 #11, measures 1-6.

"Moonlit Meadow," the concluding piece of Opus 65 (Figure 3.12), features broken-chord accompaniments in both right and left hands, as well as double notes and quiet off-beat triads. This piece could be used to teach sensitively controlled soft playing, especially playing of chords softly while voicing their top notes.

Figure 3.12. Prokofiev, "Moonlit Meadow," Opus 65 #12, measures 1-5.

Looking at the titles of Prokofiev's other piano works, it is quite probable that the two *Sonatinas,* Opus 54; the "Sonatina pastorale," Opus 59 #1; and the *Tales of the Old Grandmother,* Opus 31, were written at least partially with pedagogical intent. However, stylistically and technically they have more in common with Prokofiev's other advanced-intermediate-level works.

Advanced-intermediate-level Works

Many of Prokofiev's works for piano are suitable for students at an advanced-intermediate level. These include the following:

Four Pieces, Opus 3:	"Story," "Jest," "March," "Phantom"
Four Pieces, Opus 4:	"Reminiscence," "Elan," "Despair," "Diabolical Suggestion"
Ten Pieces, Opus 12:	"March," "Gavotte," "Rigaudon," "Mazurka," "Capriccio," "Legend," "Prelude," "Allemande," "Humoresque Scherzo," "Scherzo"

Visions fugitives, Opus 22
Tales of the Old Grandmother, Opus 31

Four Pieces, Opus 32:	"Dance," "Gavotte," "Menuet," "Waltz"
Two Sonatinas, Opus 54:	E minor and G Major
Three Pieces, Opus 59:	"Promenade," "Landscape," "Sonatina pastorale"

Inclusion of works in this list should not necessarily preclude the possibility of their performance as concert pieces, however.

Four Pieces, Opus 3

Of the *Four Pieces,* Opus 3, the most interesting is probably the "Phantom," Opus 3 #4 (Figure 3.13), an ominous piece in the unusual meter of 5/8. Marked "Presto tenebroso," this piece begins pianissimo and una corda and employs strange chromatic harmonies over an angular ostinato. After a four-measure outburst marked "fortissimo" and "tre corde," the material of the "A" section is reworked with a brief coda that ends "smorzando," suggesting the mysterious disappearance of a phantom.

Figure 3.13. Prokofiev, "Phantom," Opus 3 #4, measures 1-3.

The "March," Opus 3 #3 (Figure 3.14), marked "Allegro energico," is a strongly rhythmic piece, an ironic parody of a traditional four-square march. The harmony of this piece is bitingly dissonant, full of parallelism and, depending on the method of analysis, either polytonality or harmonic side-slipping. This piece ends, however, with as solid a V^7-I cadence in F major as could be desired. Some of the leaps from chord to chord are quite difficult.

Figure 3.14. Prokofiev, "March," Opus 3 #3, measures 1-2.

"Jest" or "Badinage," Opus 3 #2 (Figure 3.15), is a lively scherzo with some tricky staccato double-notes in the right-hand part and broken triads in the left-hand part. The contrasting legato middle-section contains a few measures in which "piano" and "forte" dynamic markings alternate on every beat with rapid crescendi and diminuendi in between.

Figure 3.15. Prokofiev, "Jest" or "Badinage," Opus 3 #2, measures 1-2.

"Story," Opus 3 #1 (Figure 3.16), is perhaps the least interesting musically of this set, despite the fact that it offers the most variety of texture. It begins rather simply, quietly, and lyrically, but builds to a rather difficult and ponderous chordal climax in the middle. Prokofiev has woven in some chromatic inner lines and harmonic alterations, but the melodic material seems rather uninspired. Some wide stretches in this piece would make it rather difficult for small hands.

Figure 3.16. Prokofiev, "Story," Opus 3 #1, measures 1-2.

Four Pieces, Opus 4

Of the *Four Pieces,* Opus 4, the "Diabolical Suggestion," Opus 4 #4 (Figure 3.17), is the most exciting, the most technically difficult, and the most popular; it certainly belongs in the repertoire of artists as well as advanced-intermediate students. The technical difficulties of this piece include trills performed by rapid alternation of hands, scale and arpeggio figures, staccato chords and thirds, rapid leaps, hand-crossing, and glissandi. Much of the writing in this piece calls for a sharply percussive staccato touch. Rhythmic intensity and excitement are required in the pianissimo leggiero sections, as well as in the rapid crescendi and expressionistic climaxes.

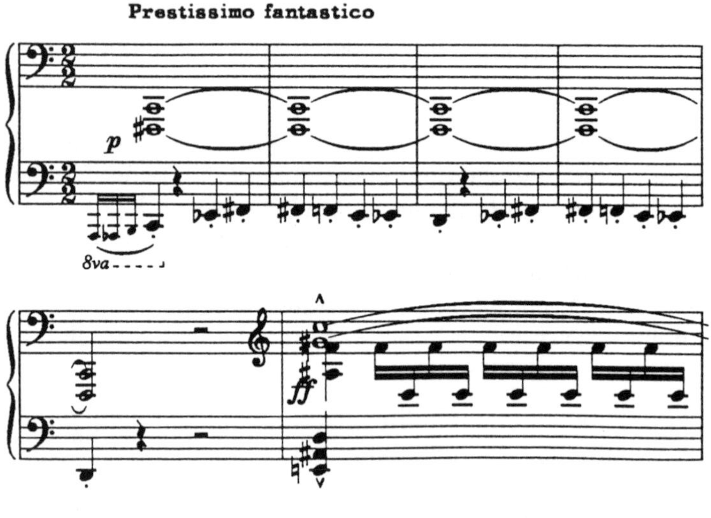

Figure 3.17. Prokofiev, "Diabolical Suggestion," Opus 4 #4, measures 1-6.

Of the remaining pieces of Opus 4, "Elan," Opus 4 #2 (Figure 3.18), may be recommended as a rhythmically dynamic study in a fast 6/8 meter. It calls for a few rapid leaps as well as some contrapuntal control of soprano and alto voices in the right hand.

Figure 3.18. Prokofiev, "Elan," Opus 4 #2, measures 1-4.

Prokofiev has prefaced "Despair," Opus 4 #3 (Figure 3.19), with the emotionally charged direction "Andante con agitazione e dolore." Built primarily over a chromatically descending three-note ostinato, the music alternately builds to a forte or fortissimo climax and subsides to a piano or pianissimo. Technically, there are some large leaps and many changes of hand position and texture, but these occur at a moderately slow tempo. Musically, this piece is a study in voicing, balance, and control of dynamics.

Figure 3.19. Prokofiev, "Despair," Opus 4 #3, measures 1-4.

"Remembrance," Opus 4 #1 (Figure 3.20), seems, like "Story" from Opus 1, to lack melodic inspiration. Prokofiev offers some intriguing harmonic, rhythmic, and textural complexities, but the overall style is apt to sound dated to modern ears. The pervasive two-against-three polyrhythm of the second half of this piece could make it useful as an etude in the style of Scriabin.

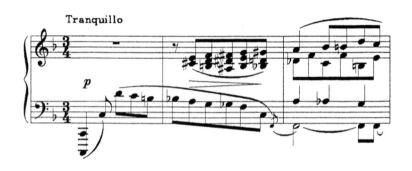

Figure 3.20. Prokofiev, "Remembrance," Opus 4 #1, measures 1-3.

Ten Pieces, Opus 12

The *Ten Pieces,* Opus 12, contain two of Prokofiev's most popular advanced-intermediate-level pieces: the "Gavotte" in G minor and the "Prelude" in C Major. Many other attractive works also belong to this opus.

Some of Prokofiev's most graceful and lyrical melodies are to be found in the "Gavotte" in G minor, Opus 12 #2 (Figure 3.21). The popularity of this piece, however, probably owes more to the resemblance to Tschaikovsky than to its touches of Prokofiev in harmony or texture.[48] Like many of Prokofiev's early pieces, this gavotte begins simply and becomes disproportionately difficult as it progresses.

Figure 3.21. Prokofiev, "Gavotte," Opus 12 #2, measures 1-2.
Figures 3.21. through 3.30., from Opus 12, reprinted
by permission of Boosey and Hawkes, Inc.

The "Prelude" in C, Opus 12 #7, has attained considerable popularity, both in its original version for solo harp, and in its transcribed form as a piano solo (Figure 3.22). The "A" section of this prelude is a valuable right-hand study requiring quiet execution of broken four-note-chord patterns. Notable in the "B" section are the pianissimo glissandi that add a touch of graceful delicacy.

Figure 3.22. Prokofiev, "Prelude," Opus 12 #7, measures 1-3.

The harmonies of the "March" in F minor, Opus 12 #1 (Figure 3.23), bite less dissonantly than those of the earlier "March," Opus 3 #3. The main theme also begins much more quietly although it is restated "fff" at the climax. Technically, the performer must contend with some leaps from chord to chord, stretches of a ninth, and two rapid F-minor scales.

Figure 3.23. Prokofiev, "March," Opus 12 #1, measures 1-3.

The "Rigaudon" in C, Opus 12 #3 (Figure 3.24), is a lively neo-Classical dance-piece that contains many clever harmonic twists and surprising modulations. It begins diatonically, but later introduces more complex chromatic writing.

Figure 3.24. Prokofiev, "Rigaudon," Opus 12 #3, measures 1-2.

Prokofiev's "Mazurka" in B, Opus 12 #4 (Figure 3.25), is more than just an experiment in which the right and left hand parts each move in parallel perfect fourths. This mazurka combines a variety of melodies, rhythms, and articulations within a well-organized formal design characterized by strong climaxes and clearly defined phrases. It could be used to introduce a theoretically minded student to parallel fourths and to teach him or her to read fluently in the key of B major.

Figure 3.25. Prokofiev, "Mazurka," Opus 12 #4, measures 1-2.

A less compelling piece is the "Capriccio," Opus 12 #5 (Figure 3.26). It moves along mainly in eighth notes at a moderate "Allegretto" tempo with occasional agitation of the tempo at climaxes. Most of the interest is provided by melodic and harmonic twists, and by the addition of counter-melodies and arpeggios in the section that contains the main climax (measures 65-88).

Figure 3.26. Prokofiev, "Capriccio," Opus 12 #5, measures 1-2.

"Legend," Opus 12 #6 (Figure 3.27), with its many parallel fifths, unusual melodic cadences, and chromatic harmonies, is reminiscent of the shorter pieces of Scriabin. In "Legend," Prokofiev has taken care to indicate the many changes of tempo, accelerandi, and ritardandi necessary for its performance. Except for some large stretches in the central "Andante religioso" section, this piece does not reach technically beyond the advanced-intermediate level.

Figure 3.27. Prokofiev, "Legend," Opus 12 #6, measures 1-2.

The "Allemande," Opus 12 #8 (Figure 3.28), curiously parodies the graceful Baroque allemande through a ponderous march-like opening theme that returns fortissimo, and through extensive use of the bass register of the piano.

This allemande presents a wide array of dynamics, textures, and registers. Also, Prokofiev introduces some enjoyable grace notes and hand-crossings when varying the themes of this allemande.

Figure 3.28. Prokofiev, "Allemande," Opus 12 #8, measures 1-3.

Originally written for four bassoons, the "Humoresque Scherzo," Opus 12 #9 (Figure 3.29), never rises above the "A" above middle C. The low register, harmonic and melodic surprises, staccato articulations, grace notes, and motivic dialogues all contribute to the grotesque humor of the "A" section. A "poco piu lento" section temporarily interrupts the mood with more serious and sustained four-part writing before a return to the humorous elements of the "A" section. The *grotesquerie* in this piece may perhaps intrigue an advanced-intermediate student.

Figure 3.29. Prokofiev, "Humoresque Scherzo," Opus 12 #9, measures 1-3.

By far the most technically demanding piece of Opus 12 is the "Scherzo" in A minor, Opus 12 #10 (Figure 3.30). As the tenth and last piece, this piece could provide a bravura conclusion to a performance of the complete opus or selections therefrom. The A-minor "Scherzo" is essentially a perpetual-motion etude in scales, broken chords, and leaps, plus occasional double notes, octaves, or contrapuntal division of the right hand. It bears a certain resemblance to Chopin's B-flat-minor "Prelude," Opus 28 #19.

Figure 3.30. Prokofiev, "Scherzo," Opus 12 #10, measures 5-8.

Visions fugitives, Opus 22

Visions fugitives, Opus 22, a suite of twenty brief pieces, takes its title from a poem by the Russian poet Konstantin Balmont, "In every fugitive vision I see worlds/Full of the changing play of rainbow hues."[49]

The Visions fugitives may be performed as a suite, or the performer may prefer to select a group of pieces, since some are more effective than others. Prokofiev has arranged these pieces in order so that the ending of one piece leads smoothly into the beginning of the next, although the links between movements are often extremely subtle (Figure 3.31).[50]

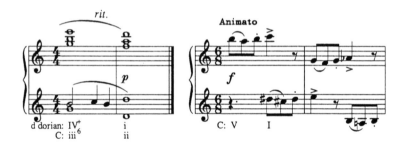

Figure 3.31. Prokofiev, "Vision fugitive," Opus 22 #3, measures 27-28; "Vision fugitive," Opus 22 #4, measures 1-2.
Figures 3.31. through 3.51., from Opus 22, reprinted by permission of Boosey and Hawkes, Inc.

The first of the Visions fugitives, Opus 22 #1 (Figure 3.32), quiet and ethereal throughout, bears the marking "con una simplicità espressiva." Though technically easy, it requires subtle control of balance and nuance and careful voicing of "ppp" chords in the bass register.

Figure 3.32. Prokofiev, "Vision fugitive," Opus 22 #1, measures 1-4.

The second piece of Opus 22 (Figure 3.33) features widely spaced legato broken-chord figures in the left hand that require discreet use of the damper pedal. Two "misterioso" passages call for emphasis in the right-hand of a middle voice sandwiched between two pedal points. A cadenza-like passage in measures 7-10 contains some virtuosic polychordal arpeggios. In measures 13-16 and 21-22, Prokofiev introduces a bell-like octave figure that should not be allowed to interfere with the melody.

Figure 3.33. Prokofiev, "Vision fugitive," Opus 22 #2, measures 1-4.

The third "Vision fugitive" (Figure 3.34) makes much use of legato parallel triads and fifths. The contrasting middle section with its staccatos, repeated leaps, and major-second pedal points may be played with a sense of ironic humor.

Figure 3.34. Prokofiev, "Vision fugitive," Opus 22 #3, measures 1-2.

Opus 22 #4 (Figure 3.35), marked "Animato," opens with a rather boisterous section. The next section, consisting of flowing scale passages over broken major-seventh chords, leads to a brief combination of elements from both sections. A transition leads in turn to a "Piu sostenuto" section in which a legato transformation of the opening motive is accompanied by pianissimo staccato chords. This piece challenges the performer through its presentation of a variety of moods, textures, and dynamics within the space of relatively few measures.

Figure 3.35. Prokofiev, "Vision fugitive," Opus 22 #4, measures 1-4.

In the fifth "Vision fugitive" (Figure 3.36), marked "Molto giocoso," Prokofiev has favored us with one of his wittiest inspirations. According to Ashley, synthesis of whole-tone and diatonic materials,[51] as well as harmonic and melodic side-slipping, polytonality, leaps, and syncopations combine to create a sense of mischievous and sometimes noisy fun. The presence of a fragmentary quotation from Tschaikovsky's "Dance of the Sugar-plum Fairy" in the fourth measure lends support to Ashley's thesis that this piece intentionally parodies nineteenth-century ballet music.[52]

Figure 3.36. Prokofiev, "Vision fugitive," Opus 22 #5, measures 1-4.

Opus 22 #6 (Figure 3.37), a contrapuntal essay that could easily have been scored for two violins, gives a glimpse of the elegant side of Prokofiev's art. Of special interest for the student should be the few intricate hand-crossings and the chromatic and modal harmonic shadings.

Figure 3.37. Prokofiev, "Vision fugitive," Opus 22 #6, measures 1-4.

Opus 22 #7 (Figure 3.38), subtitled "Arpa" ("harp"), also relies upon figurations that suggest an instrument other than the piano. As Ashley remarks, harmonic subtleties in this piece are created via shifting polymodality.[53]

Figure 3.38. Prokofiev, "Vision fugitive," Opus 22 #7, measures 3-5.

In Opus 22 #8 (Figure 3.39), Ashley observes that the two main themes are first presented in F-sharp dorian and A aeolian, respectively, then transposed and varied.[54] The performer needs to bring to this piece a sensitivity to lyrical melody and to balance between melody and accompaniment figures.

Figure 3.39. Prokofiev, "Vision fugitive," Opus 22 #8, measures 1-3.

Opus 22 #9 (Figure 3.40) may appear at first glance to be a brilliant study in sixteenth-note figurations. However, the marking "Allegretto tranquillo" cautions against excessive speed or brilliance. The consecutive minor tenths in this piece are notated without arpeggiation, and should be so played if the pianist's span allows.

Figure 3.40. Prokofiev, "Vision fugitive," Opus 22 #9, measures 1-2.

Prokofiev's sense of irony becomes immediately apparent in the direction "Ridicolosamente" that prefaces the tenth "Vision fugitive" (Figure 3.41). There is perhaps a hint of military parody in the combination of march-like rhythmic precision with melodic distortions and bitonal harmonies.

Figure 3.41. Prokofiev, "Vision fugitive," Opus 22 #10, measures 1-4.

Opus 22 #11 (Figure 3.42) begins by exploiting the peculiar rhythmic effect created by frequent accentuation of the weaker beats of the measure (beats two and four in 4/4 meter). The lyrical "B" section of this piece requires expressive cantabile playing, especially since the melody is given almost no harmonic support.

Figure 3.42. Prokofiev, "Vision fugitive," Opus 22 #11, measures 1-2.

Opus 22 #12 (Figure 3.43) is perhaps more interesting theoretically than musically, since, as Ashley points out, each of the four voices in the opening theme has a different tonal center.[55] It provides a fleeting vision of a strange waltz that remains quiet, moderate in tempo, and, despite two treacherous-looking flourishes, moderate in difficulty as well. The performer of this piece will need to pay careful attention to balance and gradation of tone in quiet playing.

Figure 3.43. Prokofiev, "Vision fugitive," Opus 22 #12, measures 1-5.

Although the "Vision fugitive," Opus 22 #13 (Figure 3.44), begins and ends simply, measures 14-21 introduce trills against counterpoint in the same hand, a challenge that may prove too difficult for most intermediate students. The cryptic chromaticism, strange ostinatos, and extensive use of trills in this piece suggest the influence of Scriabin's mysticism.

Figure 3.44. Prokofiev, "Vision fugitive," Opus 22 #13, measures 1-5.

Any hint of mysticism is exploded in Opus 22 #14 (Figure 3.45), a vigorous and almost bombastic piece marked "Feroce." This piece demands, above all, precision of rhythmic accentuation and articulation and dramatic changes in dynamics. Its technical difficulties, including rapid hand-crossing and changes of hand position, place it at the advanced-intermediate, or perhaps even advanced level.

Figure 3.45. Prokofiev, "Vision fugitive," Opus 22 #14, measures 1-4.

Opus 22 #15 (Figure 3.46), marked "Inquieto," shows a certain resemblance in its opening thematic idea to Chopin's "Prelude" in G-sharp minor, Opus 28 #16. Restless and dramatic, it gives the performer an opportunity to sustain a sense of suspense and excitement. Technically, it could serve as a study in solid triads, repeated notes, and occasional octave passages.

Figure 3.46. Prokofiev, "Vision fugitive," Opus 22 #15, measures 1-3.

Opus 22 #16 (Figure 3.47) begins with a theme in which the right hand must be placed under the left. A sensitive study in lyricism and cantabile playing, it calls occasionally for use of the sostenuto as well as the damper pedal.

Figure 3.47. Prokofiev, "Vision fugitive," Opus 22 #16, measures 1-4.

"Vision fugitive," Opus 22 #17 (Figure 3.48), legato and subdued, features a primary theme in the left hand under a right-hand ostinato. It ends with a passage consisting of slow tremolos in both hands.

Figure 3.48. Prokofiev, "Vision fugitive," Opus 22 #17, measures 5-8.

Opus 22 #18 (Figure 3.49), a slow waltz, relies largely upon tortuous wide-ranging melodies and chromatic inner lines. Though not one of the more memorable pieces in this opus, it makes intriguing and novel use of chromaticism and modality.

Figure 3.49. Prokofiev, "Vision fugitive," Opus 22 #18, measures 1-4.

Opus 22 #19, "Presto agitatissimo e molto accentuato" (Figure 3.50), remains the only piano work of Prokofiev to have been given a programmatic explanation by its composer.   Its angular melodies, syncopations, surging crescendi and diminuendi, and vehement climax create an atmosphere of tension that, according to Prokofiev, depicted the agitation of the crowds during the Russian Revolution.[56]

Figure 3.50. Prokofiev, "Vision fugitive," Opus 22 #19, measures 1-3.

The final "Vision fugitive," Opus 22 #20 (Figure 3.51), begins with eight measures of 9/8 in the right hand against 3/4 in the left, after which the left hand adapts to 9/8 meter. A mystical piece that contains motives and textures reminiscent of Scriabin's seventh *Sonata*, it serves as a quiet epilogue to the *Visions fugitives*.

Figure 3.51. Prokofiev, "Vision fugitive," Opus 22 #20, measures 1-3.

Tales of the Old Grandmother, Opus 31

Tales of the Old Grandmother, Opus 31, is a collection of four short pieces similar in style to several of the *Visions fugitives.* Because of their subdued character and their lack of technical difficulty, *Tales of the Old Grandmother* may be a collection particularly well suited for the adult advanced-intermediate student.

The first piece of Opus 31 (Figure 3.52) begins with a procession in moderate tempo, reminiscent of the "March of the Hunters" from *Peter and the Wolf.*

The "B" section, "con una dolcezza sostenuto," has a melody in the treble accompanied by low bass chords, an unusual spacing that recalls similar passages in Beethoven's late sonatas.

Figure 3.52. Prokofiev, *Tales of the Old Grandmother,* Opus 31 #1, measures 1-5.
Figures 3.52. through 3.55., from Opus 31, reprinted by permission of
Boosey and Hawkes, Inc.

The second piece of Opus 31 (Figure 3.53) has a certain kinship with "Vision fugitive," Opus 22 #8, with which it shares the tonic note of F-sharp and the use of an octave leap at the beginning of the main theme. Because of the quiet dynamic levels in this piece, balance of melody, counter-melody, and accompaniment ought again to merit careful attention.

Figure 3.53. Prokofiev, *Tales of the Old Grandmother*, Opus 31 #2, measures 1-4.

The third "Tale of the Old Grandmother," Opus 31 #3 (Figure 3.54), begins in low register, rather like a melody for violoncello accompanied by paired bassoons. After the principal melody is repeated an octave higher, the "B" section appears, featuring melodies based upon chromatic scale fragments, as well as some imitation.

Figure 3.54. Prokofiev, *Tales of the Old Grandmother*, Opus 31 #3, measures 1-3.

The concluding piece of this set, Opus 31 #4 (Figure 3.55), shows impressionistic influences in its parallelisms and in its modal melodies. The "B" section in 12/8 depends primarily upon broken-chord figurations that lie comfortably under the hand.

Figure 3.55. Prokofiev, *Tales of the Old Grandmother*, Opus 31 #4, measures 1-3.

Four Pieces, Opus 32

Prokofiev based each of the *Four Pieces*, Opus 32, upon a different dance rhythm. The first, entitled "Dance," shows possible derivation from the tango, while the others are clearly a minuet, gavotte, and waltz, respectively. Except for the rather difficult waltz, the dance pieces in this opus could serve as teaching pieces for intermediate-level students.

The "Dance," Opus 32 #1 (Figure 3.56), commences, as Ashley observes, with a theme somewhat akin to that of Debussy's "Minstrels."[57] The second section, more texturally complex than the first, requires careful pedalling in order to sustain notes which the hands cannot sustain. Technically, some of the later passages call for left-hand leaps and control of a melody and pedal-point, or of two independent lines played by the same hand. The coda is cleverly built over a V-I ostinato marked "quasi timpani."

Figure 3.56. Prokofiev, "Dance," Opus 32 #1, measures 1-2. Figures 3.56. through 3.59., from Opus 32, reprinted by permission of Boosey and Hawkes, Inc.

The "Minuet," Opus 32 #2 (Figure 3.57), demonstrates Prokofiev's skill in modernizing old dances, and could serve as a good introduction to his neo-Classical style. Written in four-bar phrases throughout, it presents some of Prokofiev's characteristic harmonic parallelisms and substitutions, together with effective contrasts of register, texture, and articulation.

Figure 3.57. Prokofiev, "Minuet," Opus 32 #2, measures 1-4.

The "Gavotte," Opus 32 #3 (Figure 3.58), accidentally labelled a waltz in an early edition, comes across as ironically neo-Classical, yet less humorous than the "Gavotte" from the *"Classical"* *Symphony*. While harmonic side-slipping and Neapolitan triads figure strongly in the "A" section, the "B" section concentrates on the melodic play of D major versus D minor and shows some whole-tone melodic influence.

Figure 3.58. Prokofiev, "Gavotte," Opus 32 #3, measures 1-3.

The "Waltz," Opus 32 #4 (Figure 3.59), accidentally labelled a gavotte in an early edition, will perhaps strike the present-day listener as an experiment in schmaltzy chromaticism. An advanced-intermediate or advanced student who finds this piece to his or her taste, however, will discover many luscious chord progressions and rich textures. Technically, this rather difficult piece features several points of hand-crossing and some widely-spaced melodies and accompaniments that lie rather awkwardly under the hand.

Figure 3.59. Prokofiev, "Waltz," Opus 32 #4, measures 1-3.

Two Sonatinas, Opus 54

Prokofiev's three sonatinas for piano all date from his foreign period (1918-1935). Of the three, two were published as Opus 54, and a third, the "Sonatina Pastorale," was published as Opus 59 #3.

The first "Sonatina" of Opus 54 (Figure 3.60), shows the influences of *Les Six* and of Stravinsky, yet appears to lack the wit one might expect from a composition in which Prokofiev imitates these composers.

Figure 3.60. Prokofiev, "Sonatina," Opus 54 #1, first movement, measures 1-4.
Figures 3.60. and 3.61., from Opus 54, reprinted by permission of Boosey and Hawkes, Inc.

In the first movement of Opus 54 #1, the irregular lengths of phrases and motives, meter changes, bitonal counterpoint, dissonant inverted pedals, and occasionally strident climaxes tend to give an overall impression of arbitrariness or artificiality. However, the contrast of first and second subjects and the cadences clarify the form sufficiently that the compositional oddities come across with a certain quirky charm.

The second and third movements tend to reinforce the somewhat disconcerting impression created by the first. The second movement, like the slow movement of Stravinsky's *Sonata,* carries the tempo marking "Adagietto." It displays some figurations that could have been influenced by Stravinsky's neo-Bachian melodies, and also some cadences in which resolutions of some voices are strangely delayed.

The third movement begins rather like Granados's "Playera," as Ashley notes,[58] but seems to be composed of several loosely related, underdeveloped thematic ideas. Frequently, melodies or arpeggios seem to wander up and down or change register arbitrarily, while odd bitonal harmonies abound. Like the other movements of this sonatina, this movement deserves to be regarded perhaps as an intriguing experiment, rather than a particularly good choice for a student to learn or an artist to memorize and perform.

The second "Sonatina" of Opus 54 (Figure 3.61), by contrast, succeeds more readily in demonstrating Prokofiev's skill as a composer. The first movement of this sonatina relies upon a solid triadic harmonic foundation, with strong contrasts between themes and sections, and emphatic, sonorous climaxes between sections of calm repose.

Figure 3.61. Prokofiev, "Sonatina" in G, Opus 54 #2, measures 1-2.

As Patricia Ashley points out, the second movement of Opus 54 #2 bears a resemblance in its simplicity and discreet employment of Prokofiev's devices to some of the movements in Prokofiev's *Romeo and Juliet*.[59] The "B" section consists of a tonally wandering melody accompanied by a tonally wandering Alberti-bass pattern.

The third movement of Opus 54 #2 is probably the weakest. Oddly enough, all of the structurally important cadences end with a diminuendo and often a ritardando as well. The formal structure is weakened by overlapping of phrases and thin spacings of chords at cadences. Fortunately, sufficient rhythmic momentum and Prokofiev's use of familiar tertian chords at cadences hold the movement together.

Three Pieces, Opus 59

Prokofiev's Opus 59 consists of three pieces, entitled "Promenade," "Landscape," and "Sonatina pastorale." The "Sonatina pastorale" is probably the most appealing of the three.

Ashley points out that, except for an "Allegro moderato" coda, the various sections of the "Promenade," Opus 59 #1 (Figure 3.62), stay within a comfortable walking tempo (MM $\downarrow$ = 96 to MM $\downarrow$ = 126).[60] This piece displays stylistic traits found in several of Prokofiev's second-period pieces: relatively simple rhythms, clear tonality, free addition and subtraction of voices, and discreet use of harmonic and melodic side-slipping and chromaticism.

Figure 3.62. Prokofiev, "Promenade," Opus 59 #1, measures 1-5.
Figures 3.62. through 3.64., from Opus 59, reprinted by permission of Boosey and Hawkes, Inc.

"Landscape," Opus 59 #2 (Figure 3.63), suffers somewhat from the use of an undistinguished arpeggiated polychord for its main theme, although the quasi-palindrome structure of this theme is of some historical interest. On the positive side, its lyrical "B" theme and many subtle tempo changes encourage interpretive sensitivity to detail. This piece would probably be more useful as an intermediate-level finger-study than as a recital piece.

Figure 3.63. Prokofiev, "Landscape," Opus 59 #2, measures 1-2.

The "Sonatina pastorale" in C Major, Opus 59 #3 (Figure 3.64), a quietly lyrical piece, uses many of the devices of the first two pieces of Opus 59 within a sonata-allegro form. The secondary keys of this sonatina (B-flat, D, and A-flat) all lie within the whole-tone scale of C. The arpeggios and counterpoints produce many changes of hand position. This piece also offers cantabile melodies and much rhythmic variety.

Figure 3.64. Prokofiev, "Sonatina pastorale," Opus 59 #3, measures 1-4.

Advanced-level or Concert Works

In this category may be placed those piano works of Prokofiev that are rightfully the property of the advanced student or concert artist. Of these works, Prokofiev's series of nine sonatas certainly constitutes his most substantial contribution to the concert pianist's solo repertoire. Besides the sonatas, piano works by Prokofiev that belong in the artist's repertory include the *Etudes,* Opus 2; the *Toccata,* Opus 11; the *Sarcasms,* Opus 17; the *Choses en soi,* Opus 45; and the *Pensées,* Opus 62.

Toccata, Opus 11

Of the miscellaneous concert works, the most popular by far is the *Toccata,* Opus 11 (Figure 3.65). The Prokofiev *Toccata* is an expressionistic work demanding tremendous endurance and rhythmic drive. Technically, this work features alternate hand passages, leaps, and a glissando, as well as passages requiring control of melody and counterpoint within the same hand. Interpretively, the *Toccata* requires, above all, evenness of rhythm and steadiness of tempo in order to sustain the tension of the constant sixteenth-note pulsation.

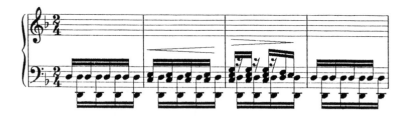

Figure 3.65. Prokofiev, *Toccata,* Opus 11, measures 9-12.

Four Etudes, Opus 2

Each of the *Etudes,* Opus 2 #1-4 [Figure 3.66 (a)-(d)] is a study in perpetual motion. The first etude begins as a study in broken-chord figures and introduces octaves in the "B" section. The second etude is a study in scale figures with polyrhythms of four notes against nine, later five notes against nine. The third etude requires rapid changes of hand position and control of two independent voices in the right-hand part. This right-hand counterpoint utilizes the pervasive rhythmic patterns ♫ ♩ against ♩ ♫. In the fourth etude, Prokofiev interjects jagged motives over a broken-octave bass.

Figure 3.66. Prokofiev, *Etudes,* (a) Opus 2 #1, measure 1; (b) Opus 2 #2, measure 1; (c) Opus 2 #3, measures 1-2; (d) Opus 2 #4, measure 1.

These etudes could provide a welcome alternative to standard nineteenth-century etude literature. Musically, the lyricism of the second etude contrasts well with the drama and drive of the other three etudes.

Sarcasms, Opus 17

The five *Sarcasms,* Opus 17, demonstrate Prokofiev's biting wit, a trait present prominently in both his personality and his art. Prokofiev sometimes complained, however, that the lyricism in his work was often overlooked in favor of the more obvious elements of irony and grotesquerie.

The first of the "Sarcasms," Opus 17 #1 (Figure 3.67), presents two strongly contrasting theme groups. The first theme group owes its "tempestoso" character to strong accents and rhythmic drive, angular melodies, repeated tritones, and a dynamic range from fortissimo to pianissimo. The second subject, a lyrical tune in the Lydian mode, soon gives way to syncopation and chromatic scales in contrary motion. Technically, this piece contains octaves, leaps, scales, contrapuntal division within the hand, and chords that require voicing of melodic inner lines.

Figure 3.67. Prokofiev, "Sarcasm," Opus 17 #1, measures 1-6.
Figures 3.67. through 3.71., from Opus 17, used with the permission of G. Schirmer, Inc., New York (ASCAP) on behalf of RAIS (Russia).

The second "Sarcasm," Opus 17 #2 (Figure 3.68), carries the surprising Italian indication of "Allegro rubato." Prokofiev generally held rubato in distaste[61] but here calls for it specifically in a quasi-improvisatory but unsentimental context. In this piece, parallel seventh chords alternate frequently with arpeggiated flourishes. Technically, the arpeggios and the final cadenza are quite difficult. Musically, because of its vaguely established tonalities, its staccato chords and accents, and its strident ending, this piece tends to come across, perhaps, as one of Prokofiev's most discordant statements.

Figure 3.68. Prokofiev, "Sarcasm," Opus 17 #2, measures 1-4.

Prokofiev's third "Sarcasm," Opus 17 #3 (Figure 3.69), lives up to its preface "Allegro precipitato" (fast and precipitously) by virtue of its fast, motoric repeated chords, sudden fortissimo outbursts, extended crescendi, and the "fff" restatement of its quiet opening theme. In the "B" section, eight measures of a syncopated melody marked "Singhiozzando" (sobbing) lead to a lyrical theme marked "un poco largamente." Technically, the motoric eighth notes and chords of the "A" section recall the "Diabolical Suggestion." Ashley remarks that, in the "Un poco largamente" section, the inner voices curiously enough are written so that the thumbs cross over each other unnecessarily.[62]

Figure 3.69. Prokofiev, "Sarcasm," Opus 17 #3, measures 1-4.

The fourth piece of Opus 17 (Figure 3.70), marked "Smanioso" (raving), bursts on the scene fortissimo with strident repeated chords and some of the most complex rhythms to be found in all of Prokofiev's piano works. The middle section requires repetition of chords against sustained melody tones within each hand. This piece ends "ppp" and "una corda" with a quiet glissando amid echoes of the opening theme.

Figure 3.70. Prokofiev, "Sarcasm," Opus 17 #4, measures 1-2.

Like the other pieces of Opus 17, the last of the *Sarcasms,* Opus 17 #5 (Figure 3.71), carries a rare Italian marking, in this case "Precipitosissimo." In the opening of this piece, Prokofiev changes meter as frequently as Bartók or Stravinsky might have done. The opening also happens to be rather strident. The "Andante" that follows first employs a witty dialogue of staccato motives and rests, then proceeds to introduce a contrasting legato melody. Technically, this piece calls for some wide stretches, as well as some hand-crossing, finger substitution, and independence of touches within the hand and between the hands.

Figure 3.71. Prokofiev, "Sarcasm," Opus 17 #5, measures 1-4.

Choses en soi, Opus 45

The first "Chose en soi," Opus 45 #1, and the three *Pensées,* Opus 62, are generally less difficult technically than the sonatas, etudes, *Toccata,* or *Sarcasms.* However, they are too long and serious in conception to fit comfortably into the category of advanced-intermediate-level pieces.

The two *Choses en soi (Things in Themselves),* Opus 45, take their titles from an abstraction of Kantian philosophy. Prokofiev evidently chose these anti-programmatic titles to warn the performer that these are pieces of absolute music.

The first "Chose en soi," Opus 45 #1, a full three hundred and fifty-three measures long, constructs its main themes from such simple motives as falling fourths plus neighbor tones (Figure 3.72):

Figure 3.72. Prokofiev, "Chose en soi," Opus 45 #1, measures 1-4.
Figures 3.72. through 3.74., from Opus 45, reprinted by permission of
Boosey and Hawkes, Inc.

or minor seconds plus three-note scale motives (Figure 3.73):

Figure 3.73. Prokofiev, "Chose en soi," Opus 45 #1, measures 21-26.

Out of these simple materials, Prokofiev derives a variety of distinct yet closely related themes.

Though little known, the first "Chose en soi" should appeal to many performers. Alternation of motoric and lyrical writing, together with contrasts of mood, dynamics, and tempo, offer the performer ample scope for interpretive variety and subtlety. The coda offers the opportunity to generate excitement as it progresses from "Piu mosso" via "un poco stringendo" to "Piu allegro," "Ancora piu mosso," and finally "con brio" with a brilliant, fortissimo conclusion. Technically, the octaves and broken-chord figurations, while not excessively difficult, are sufficiently fast and loud to sound impressive.

The second "Chose en soi," Opus 45 #2 (Figure 3.74), also a long and complex work, tends to a greater degree toward chromaticism and rhythmic intricacy than does the first. The simplicity of its opening measures belies the fact that this piece contains some of Prokofiev's most complex writing for solo piano. Themes introduced in the early sections of this work are developed and intricately varied within a fantasia-like overall structure. In the second and fourth main sections, both marked "Andante," as well as in the "Poco meno" section, Prokofiev introduces an enchanting impressionistic layering of textures that is unique in his solo piano *oeuvre*; in the "Poco meno" section, the texture even requires three staves.

Figure 3.74. Prokofiev, "Chose en soi," Opus 45 #2, measures 1-3.

In short, both of the *Choses en soi* deserve to be explored by the serious student of Prokofiev.

Pensées, Opus 62

The first of the three *Pensées,* Opus 62 #1 (Figure 3.75), opens with a rather somber "Adagio penseroso," written in quarter notes.   The ensuing "moderato" is distinguished possibly by the doubling of a wandering, chant-like melody at the fifteenth. Doubling of melody at the fifteenth appears as a device used also in the "B" section, a section in which the accompanying lines move in faster notes.   Throughout this piece, cross-relations play a prominent role harmonically.

Figure 3.75. Prokofiev, "Pensée," Opus 62 #1, measures 1-6.
Figures 3.75. through 3.77., from Opus 62, reprinted by permission of
Boosey and Hawkes, Inc.

The second "Pensée," Opus 62 #2 (Figure 3.76), explores even stranger harmonic regions than the first. This introspective piece borders on atonality, despite the use of major and minor chords at structurally important cadence points.

Figure 3.76. Prokofiev, "Pensée," Opus 62 #2, measures 1-3.

The third "Pensée," Opus 62 #3 (Figure 3.77), tends to dwell upon bitonal harmonic combinations, and the alternation of major and minor thirds. The middle section builds to a lively climax with a glimpse of the younger Prokofiev's good humor. This work is the most extensive and difficult of the *Pensées,* though none of these pieces stands out as being extremely difficult technically or especially gratifying musically.

Figure 3.77. Prokofiev, "Pensée," Opus 62 #3, measures 1-3.

Sonatas

This brings us to the *Sonatas,* arguably Prokofiev's most important contributions to the literature of the piano. As Patricia Ashley notes, Prokofiev always "approached the form [of the sonata] with extreme seriousness."[63] Each Prokofiev sonata offers unique rewards for performer and listener, although some of the sonatas are more consistently appealing than others.

The first *Sonata,* Opus 1 (Figure 3.78), written for Prokofiev's teacher Essipova, belongs to the Romantic school of pianism. As Israel Nestyev remarks, its second subject bears a close resemblance to the second subject of Schumann's *Sonata* in F minor, Opus 11.[64] Though disparaged by some critics as being stylistically derivative, this sonata nonetheless remains an effective piece that contains dramatic passages in octaves and polyrhythmic passages of two against three that should prove gratifying to the advanced student.

Figure 3.78. Prokofiev, *Sonata #1,* Opus 1, measures 1-2.

The second *Sonata,* Opus 14, despite many neo-Romantic elements, may be considered Prokofiev's first primarily neo-Classical sonata. In this work, Prokofiev synthesizes a contemporary harmonic idiom, together with a certain amount of Romantic lyricism and passion, within a tightly Classical formal structure.

While not the most difficult of the Prokofiev sonatas, the second *Sonata* ought to challenge and reward the advanced student technically and interpretively. The themes are, with few exceptions, strongly characterized; formal designs are clear and convincing; and the young Prokofiev's extroversion is evidenced by much dramatic and bravura writing.

The first movement of Opus 14 (Figure 3.79) introduces broad Romantic themes that contrast with ostinato and *stile mécanique* figures. At the climax of the development, Prokofiev contrapuntally combines the second subject with two different ostinatos taken from earlier transitional sections. Technically, this movement requires some rapid leaps, rapid changes of hand position, and legato octaves.

Figure 3.79. Prokofiev, *Sonata #2,* Opus 14, first movement, measures 1-3. Figures 3.79. through 3.82., from Opus 14, reprinted by permission of Boosey and Hawkes, Inc.

The second movement of Opus 14 (Figure 3.80), a neo-Classical scherzo originally written for Liadov's harmony class, is primarily a study in chords created by chromatic motion against pedal points. The hand-crossing passages are extremely tricky, while the many subtle alterations of chord and interval formations make the constant shifting of hand position rather awkward and difficult as well. The trio is built upon slurred figures that call for smooth movement of the arm and wrist.

Figure 3.80. Prokofiev, *Sonata #2,* Opus 14, second movement ("Scherzo"), measures 1-2.

The third movement of Opus 14 (Figure 3.81)—lyrical, Romantic, and serious in tone—provides a center of gravity for the work. The second subject, in the unusual meter of 7/8, suffers perhaps from a certain predictability; nonetheless, it does show harmonic creativity in its polytonal combinations.

Figure 3.81. Prokofiev, *Sonata #2,* Opus 14, third movement, measures 2-3.

The fourth movement of Opus 14 (Figure 3.82), an exciting neo-Classical tarantella, is soon interrupted in the exposition by a brassy second subject in 2/4. Surprisingly, too, at the height of the development section, a cyclic reprise of the second subject from the first movement occurs. Especially gratifying for the performer of this movement are: (1) the sassy humor of the second subject theme; (2) the repeated sforzando C-sharp in the development; and (3) the bravura dominant-thirteenth arpeggios in both the introduction and the coda.

Figure 3.82. Prokofiev, *Sonata #2,* Opus 14, fourth movement, measures 1-5.

The third *Sonata,* Opus 28 (Figure 3.83), like the first *Sonata,* consists of only one movement, yet the formal design of the third *Sonata* displays much greater originality. The third *Sonata* relies considerably upon sophisticated techniques of thematic development including diminution, stretto, motivic development, and rapid modulation through distantly related keys.

This sonata has earned its place among Prokofiev's most frequently performed piano works. Its success probably owes much to the steady rhythmic momentum of the first subject group, the tender lyricism of the second subject group, the variety and intricacy of its thematic development, and the powerful climaxes, especially those in the development section and the last four measures. Technically, difficulties in this sonata include arpeggiated chords; trill figures; and staccato chords, notably chains of triads in first inversion similar to those in the finale of Beethoven's *Sonata,* Opus 2 #3.

Figure 3.83. Prokofiev, *Sonata #3,* Opus 28, measures 1-2.
Reprinted by permission of Boosey and Hawkes, Inc.

The fourth *Sonata,* Opus 29 (Figure 3.84), like the third *Sonata,* bears the subtitle "From Old Notebooks." Some passages in the first two movements of the fourth *Sonata* show signs of immaturity; for example, themes in the first movement seem to lack strong harmonic direction.

Figure 3.84. Prokofiev, *Sonata #4*, Opus 29, first movement, measures 1-3.
Figures 3.84. through 3.86., from Opus 29, reprinted by permission of
Boosey and Hawkes, Inc.

The second movement of Opus 29 (Figure 3.85), transcribed
by Prokofiev from an earlier symphony in E minor, makes use of some
rather sophisticated canons at the tritone and canons in inversion.

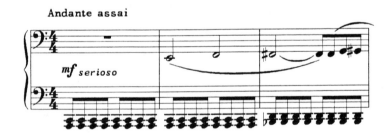

Figure 3.85. Prokofiev, *Sonata #4*, Opus 29, second movement, measures 1-3.

The third movement of Opus 29 (Figure 3.86), the last of the
three movements to be composed, surpasses the previous two
movements in thematic invention, pianistic effectiveness, and spirit. It
shows the extent to which Prokofiev's style had matured since the days

of his old notebooks. Technically, the rapid hand-over-hand scales in this movement, although they sound extremely brilliant, will probably prove less technically difficult than some of the arpeggios, widely spaced Alberti-bass patterns, and parallel quartal chords.

Figure 3.86. Prokofiev, *Sonata #4*, Opus 29, third movement, measures 1-3.

The fifth *Sonata*, Opus 38, the only sonata written during Prokofiev's foreign period, remains one of the least frequently played. In keeping with Prokofiev's foreign-period practice, which involved a deliberate departure from virtuosic display, all three movements of this sonata progress in moderate tempi. The harmonies are frequently bitonal, the textures frequently spare. Although Prokofiev revised this sonata toward the end of his life, he did so without substantial stylistic changes.

The first movement of Opus 38 (Figure 3.87) has few outstanding technical difficulties, despite some tricky polyrhythms created by the quintuplet accompaniment to the second subject, and some extended crossed-hand passages. Probably the most inspired writing is to be found in the principal theme and its return.

Figure 3.87. Prokofiev, *Sonata #5,* Opus 38, first movement, measures 1-2.
Figures 3.87. through 3.89., from Opus 38, reprinted by permission of
Boosey and Hawkes, Inc.

The second movement of Opus 38 (Figure 3.88), constructed largely over a bass of repeated eighth-note chords, employs sophisticated harmonic devices, such as brief harmonic digressions that Ashley refers to as "asides."[65] There are a few treacherous leaps, as well as several passages that require sustaining of a tone plus execution of independent motives in the same hand.

Figure 3.88. Prokofiev, *Sonata #5,* Opus 38, second movement, measures 3-6.

The third movement of Opus 38 (Figure 3.89), a rondo, begins with a simple theme of repeated notes over an Alberti bass. From this quiet beginning, Prokofiev leads the performer through contrasting themes and textures to an emphatic climax built upon parallel chords, broken octaves and motoric sixteenth-note patterns.

Figure 3.89. Prokofiev, *Sonata #5,* Opus 38, third movement, measures 1-3.

The sixth, seventh, and eighth *Sonatas* were written concurrently during World War II and were finished in 1940, 1942, and 1944, respectively. These three sonatas show evidence of Prokofiev's return to neo-Romanticism and even expressionism.

The first movement of the sixth *Sonata,* Opus 82 (Figure 3.90), seizes the listener's attention immediately with its conflict of A major versus A minor, plus its principal motive of descending major thirds, a motive that recurs in various guises in the first, third, and fourth movements. Like the third *Sonata,* the first movement of the sixth *Sonata* depends, through much of its length, upon motivic development, including augmentation and combination of motives. The development section, the longest section in this movement, has a tendency perhaps to rely too heavily upon repeated notes.

Portions of the first movement of Opus 82 reflect the turbulence of wartime. In measures 141, 145 and 148, Prokofiev directs the performer to play "col pugno" (with the fist), a direction that, although noted by Kinsey,[66] is surprisingly absent from several editions.

In this movement, Prokofiev also challenges the performer with glissandi, dangerous leaps, and hand-crossing, in addition to scales, arpeggios, and trill figures.

Figure 3.90. Prokofiev, *Sonata #6*, Opus 82, first movement, measures 1-2.
Figures 3.90. through 3.93., from Opus 82, used with the permission of G. Schirmer, Inc., New York (ASCAP) on behalf of RAIS (Russia).

The second movement of Opus 82 (Figure 3.91), a rather genial march-like scherzo, demonstrates the gentler side of Prokofiev's sense of humor through its lightness of touch, underscored by sophisticated irregularity of phrasing and dialogue of registers. A series of arpeggio figures, each with a wide gap in the middle (measures 36-42, 49-56, and 130-136) presents the only significant technical difficulty in this movement.

Figure 3.91. Prokofiev, *Sonata #6*, Opus 82, second movement, measures 1-4.

The third movement of Opus 82, "Tempo di valzer lentissimo" (Figure 3.92), is a stylized waltz in 9/8 that perhaps betrays the influence of sentimental popular music. An effective performance of this movement requires the ability to sustain a continuous waltz feeling at a very slow tempo. The middle section, "Poco piu animato," contains some passages of suspended harmonic motion (measures 42-44, 67-69) that could easily become static without dynamic direction added by the performer. The middle section also introduces a new variation on the major-third motif (mm. 71-77).

Figure 3.92. Prokofiev, *Sonata #6*, Opus 82, third movement, measures 1-2.

The lively, spirited finale of the sixth *Sonata*, Opus 82 (Figure 3.93), is characterized by thin textures and contrasts of concise motives with broader themes. In the development of the finale, quotes from the first subject and development section of the first movement reappear. Toward the end of this movement, Prokofiev dwells upon dialogues between fragments of the first subjects from the first and last movements.

Figure 3.93. Prokofiev, *Sonata #6*, Opus 82, fourth movement, measures 1-2.

Prokofiev's sixth *Sonata,* Opus 82, may certainly be recommended as a concert piece, the only drawback being occasional repetitiousness and extended sections of motivic development that could create a lack of direction. Any such weakness, nonetheless, could be minimized in performance by a strong sense of dramatic and rhythmic continuity.

The seventh *Sonata,* Opus 83, stands as probably the most technically demanding and the most consistently effective of the Prokofiev sonatas.

The first movement of Opus 83 (Figure 3.94) contrasts an "Allegro inquieto" first subject-group with an "Andantino" second subject-group. The "Allegro inquieto" creates an atmosphere of nervous excitement through driving 6/8 rhythms, stretti, chromatically altered chords, and predominantly staccato touch. The "Andantino" provides an uneasy respite with its angular counterpoint that occasionally verges on atonality. A thirty-measure accelerando leads from the "Andantino" back to the original tempo and to a development section marked by violent climaxes and lightning-quick leaps. After a truncated recapitulation of the first subject group and a full recapitulation of the second, a coda further develops the motives of the first subject group.

Figure 3.94. Prokofiev, *Sonata #7,* Opus 83, first movement, measures 1-4.
Figures 3.94. through 3.96., from Opus 83, used with the permission of G. Schirmer, Inc., New York (ASCAP) on behalf of RAIS (Russia).

The principal theme of the second movement of Opus 83 (Figure 3.95) shows perhaps a popular-music influence and affords the performer an opportunity to indulge in Romantic sentimentality. The "B" section reaches a climax that resounds like the tolling of great bells (measures 53-59, 62-64). Ghostly echoes of this climax create a particularly hypnotic effect (measures 79-86).

Andante caloroso

Figure 3.95. Prokofiev, *Sonata #7,* Opus 83, second movement, measures 1-3.

The third movement of Opus 83 (Figure 3.96), an expressionistic toccata to end all expressionistic toccatas, creates at times an almost unbearable tension, particularly in the repeated dominant-ninth chords of the last few pages. The 7/8 (2+3+2) meter,

8

quite difficult to maintain, supplies a metrical asymmetry that, together with the asymmetry of phrasing, imparts a particular feeling of being on edge. The E-minor episode (measures 79-100) gives a temporary comic relief without a relaxation of the rhythmic drive. On the last few pages, the leaps, being extremely fast and somewhat awkward, require a certain fearlessness or blind trust in the ability of the body to respond instantly to musical imagery. This toccata may be recommended without reservation to the pianist in search of a brilliant finale for a solo piano recital.

Figure 3.96. Prokofiev, *Sonata #7*, Opus 83, third movement, measures 1-3.

The eighth *Sonata,* Opus 84, unlike the other "war" sonatas, begins with a predominantly reflective, lyrical first movement. The peaceful mood of the first movement (Figure 3.97) is disturbed by obsessive repetition of the figure ♫. and by climaxes rivalling those of the seventh *Sonata* in volume and difficulty.

Figure 3.97. Prokofiev, *Sonata #8,* Opus 84, first movement, measures 1-2.
Figures 3.97. through 3.99., from Opus 84, used with the permission of G. Schirmer, Inc., New York (ASCAP) on behalf of RAIS (Russia).

The second movement of Opus 84, "Andante sognando" (Figure 3.98), provides a mature example of the "Prokofievized" minuet. The repetition of the charming opening theme up a half-step might have reduced this movement to a banal popular serenade were it not for Prokofiev's craftsmanship, evident throughout the movement.

Figure 3.98. Prokofiev, *Sonata #8,* Opus 84, second movement, measures 1-3.

The third movement of Opus 84 (Figure 3.99), offers the most immediate appeal through its lively gigue-like principal theme, its playfully menacing use of staccato in low register, and its bustling motoric patterns of eighth notes, triplet eighths, and two-against-three. The middle section, a pesante waltz, suffers somewhat, as Ashley remarks, from repetition of a basic motive Ab-G-(G)-Ab seventy-eight times,[67] although Prokofiev evidently expected the performer to use this motive to build tension within this section. Before the "A" section returns, a motivicallly related theme from the first movement reappears (mm. 289-342), creating polymetric counterpoint. In the coda, octaves, leaps, and trumpet-like repeated notes add to the excitement.

Figure 3.99. Prokofiev, *Sonata #8,* Opus 84, third movement, measures 1-2.

The eighth *Sonata* remains somewhat less popular than the sixth or seventh, presumably because of the more subdued nature of its opening movement. Still, this sonata has been singled out with special affection by one of Prokofiev's favorite interpreters, the pianist Sviatoslav Richter.[68]

The ninth *Sonata*, Opus 103, written in 1947, stands out among the sonatas for its simplicity, clarity, and relative lack of virtuosic technical difficulties. In this sonata, we also find a unique kind of reverse cyclic form, in which the coda of each movement anticipates the theme of the following movement, with the exception of the coda of the last movement, which recalls the opening theme of the sonata.

The first movement of the ninth *Sonata* (Figure 3.100) has a predominantly tranquil mood, interrupted by two fortissimo outbursts, one in the development and one in the coda. Though rather non-dramatic in technique and dynamics, this movement nonetheless presents some serenely lyrical themes and a few oddities, for example, a melody doubled at the ninth (measures 65-67).

Figure 3.100. Prokofiev, *Sonata #9*, Opus 103, first movement, measures 1-2.
Figures 3.100. through 3.103., from Opus 103, used with the permission of G. Schirmer, Inc., New York (ASCAP) on behalf of RAIS (Russia).

The second movement of Opus 103, "Allegro strepitoso" (Figure 3.101), is a march that features several scale patterns in triplets. The trio makes special use of two-part counterpoint; as one commentator remarks, Prokofiev's skillful two-voice writing often "produces passages of a balanced clarity not often heard in contemporary counterpoint."[69]

Figure 3.101. Prokofiev, *Sonata #9*, Opus 103, second movement, measures 1-2.

The third movement of Opus 103, "Andante tranquillo" (Figure 3.102), opens, like the slow movements of the seventh and eighth *Sonatas*, with a rather sentimental tune. Curiously, in the first few measures, the right-hand melody and left-hand accompaniment often share notes in a way that would tend to make the player wish for a piano with two manuals.[70] This movement follows a rondo form with two "Allegro sostenuto" episodes entering between statements of the "Andante tranquillo" theme.

Figure 3.102. Prokofiev, *Sonata #9*, Opus 103, third movement, measures 1-2.

The spirited finale of Opus 103, "Allegro con brio, ma non troppo presto" (Figure 3.103), succeeds in conveying a lively mood through energetic rhythms, harmonic surprises, and contrasting articulations. When the theme of the first movement returns in the coda, Prokofiev introduces polyrhythms of five notes against two.

Figure 3.103. Prokofiev, *Sonata #9*, Opus 103, fourth movement, measures 1-2.

The ninth *Sonata,* Opus 103, remains rather neglected, not so much because of glaring defects, but because it lacks the effectiveness of most of the earlier sonatas in the area of technical display and thematic invention. This sonata could, however, serve as an excellent recital piece for an advanced student with limited technical facility.

Prokofiev had apparently planned to convert the two *Sonatinas,* Opus 54, into his tenth and eleventh sonatas, though he was unable to complete this project before his death. When we consider the brain concussion he received in 1945 and the subsequent deterioration of his health, we should count ourselves fortunate that he was sufficiently strong-willed to complete the ninth *Sonata.*

Transcriptions

A fourth, largely unexplored area of Prokofiev's solo piano *oeuvre* consists of the many transcriptions he made of his own works and works by other composers. A list of these transcriptions includes the following:

Opus 25:	*"Classical" Symphony* (No. 1) in D Major
Opus 33-ter:	March" and "Scherzo"
	from *The Love for Three Oranges*
Opus 43-bis:	*Divertimento*
Opus 52:	*Six Transcriptions*
Opus 67:	*Peter and the Wolf*
Opus 75:	*Ten Pieces from "Romeo and Juliet"*
Opus 77-bis:	*"Gavotte" from Hamlet*
Opus 95:	*Three Pieces for Piano from "Cinderella"*
Opus 96:	*Three Pieces from "War and Peace"*
	and "Lermontov":
	#1, "Waltz" from *War and Peace;*
	#2, "Contredanse" from *Lermontov;*
	#3, "Mephisto Waltz" from *Lermontov*
Opus 97:	*Ten Pieces for Piano from "Cinderella"*
Opus 102:	*Six Pieces for Piano from "Cinderella"*
Organ *Fugue* in D minor (Buxtehude)	
Waltzes (Schubert)	

It can be seen from this list that the majority of Prokofiev's transcriptions for piano come from his ballets, with the rest taken mainly from orchestral works or from the independent instrumental sections of his operas. Only two are taken from the works of other composers. It should also be apparent that most of his transcriptions were published during the Soviet period.

Prokofiev's transcriptions serve several purposes:

1) They give the pianist an opportunity to become intimately acquainted with music from Prokofiev's orchestral works, operas, and ballets. In this regard, they may be useful either as study scores or as reading material.

2)   By following Prokofiev's piano transcriptions while listening to orchestral recordings, the student may gain an appreciation of Prokofiev's skill as an orchestrator, and may transfer that knowledge to the interpretation of his solo piano works.

3)   By following the ballet and opera transcriptions while watching videotapes of stage productions of these works, the student may also enrich his or her dramatic imagination and sense of musical gesture, especially as it affects the interpretation of Prokofiev's works.

4)   Many of these transcriptions would serve well as independent recital pieces, providing an alternative to more frequently performed works.

Opus 25, transcription of "Classical" Symphony

Prokofiev's transcription for piano of his *"Classical" Symphony,* Opus 25 (Figure 3.104), bears the same opus number as its orchestral counterpart.

Prokofiev once remarked that he wanted to write the kind of symphony that Haydn would have written had he lived into the twentieth century.[71] The result was the *"Classical" Symphony,* a work that remains one of the early milestones of neo-Classicism, even though it leaves the question unanswered as to what Haydn actually would have written had he been composing in 1920.

Prokofiev's transcription of this symphony bears the marks of a study score, rather than a concert piece. In the second and fourth movements, Prokofiev has added, on a third stave in small print, those orchestral counterpoints that could not be included in an arrangement for two hands alone.

Although, by ignoring the counterpoints in small notes, this transcription could conceivably be performed in concert, the pianistic writing would still exhibit certain weaknesses. The repeated chords in the first and second movements do not work well on the piano. Also, the awkwardness of many of the leaps, stretches, and arpeggiated chords, as well as the thinness of many of the textures, would be difficult to disguise. Of the four movements, the transcription of the "Gavotte" remains the simplest and the most suitable for performance in its transcribed form.

Figure 3.104. Prokofiev, Opus 25, transcription for piano of
"Classical" Symphony in D, first movement, measures 1-3.
Reprinted by permission of Boosey and Hawkes, Inc.

Opus 33-ter, two transcriptions from Love for Three Oranges

Prokofiev chose to publish transcriptions of the two most popular orchestral excerpts from his most successful opera, *Love for Three Oranges* (Opus 33). The popular success of this opera in its Chicago debut season was so great that the Sunkist™ orange company even tried to persuade Prokofiev to endorse their product.[72]

The "March" from *Love for Three Oranges,* (Figure 3.105), which serves in the opera to accompany the King and Queen of Clubs and their court, fares well in transcription, despite the loss of orchestral color. There are a few notes that cannot be properly connected on the piano (measures 16-17), but otherwise the spacings, repeated notes, and scale figures are pianistically effective.

Tempo di Marcia

Figure 3.105. Prokofiev, Opus 33-ter, transcription of the "March"
from *Love for Three Oranges*, measures 2-4.
Figures 3.105. and 3.106., from Opus 33-ter, reprinted by permission of
Boosey and Hawkes, Inc.

Prokofiev's transcription of the "Scherzo" from *Love for Three Oranges* (Figure 3.106) succeeds well as a piano piece. Even the occasional widely spaced sonorities are not atypical of sonorities found in Prokofiev's solo piano music or Beethoven's late sonatas. This transcription should appeal to performer and listener through its brisk tarantella tempo, spicy harmonies and modulations, exciting crescendi and dynamic contrasts, and many flourishes, including a rapid glissando.

Allegro con brio

Figure 3.106. Prokofiev, Opus 33-ter, transcription of the "Scherzo"
from *Love for Three Oranges*, measures 9-11.

Opus 43-bis, transcription of Divertimento

The *Divertimento,* Opus 43-bis (Figure 3.107), transcribed by the composer from an orchestral work bearing the same name (Opus 43), dates from the foreign period and shows the influence of *Les Six* and Stravinsky. In the first movement, marked "Molto ritmato," a repeated-chord motive interrupts the flow of the music periodically (at measures 42-45, 100-103, 107-109, 116-119), recalling similar repeated-chord motives in Stravinsky's *Rite of Spring.* The second movement, a lyrical "Larghetto," is followed by an "Allegro energico" scherzo, which begins in the low register of the piano, and features many parallel ninths. The scherzo is followed by a spirited finale, marked "Allegro non troppo e pesante." This transcription bears the marks of a study score, including orchestral scoring abbreviations, as well as extra parts written in small print above the staff at several points in the score.

Figure 3.107. Prokofiev, Opus 43-bis, transcription of *Divertimento,* first movement, measures 1-3. Reprinted by permission of Boosey and Hawkes, Inc.

Opus 52, Six Transcriptions for Piano

In 1931, Prokofiev published six transcriptions for piano as his Opus 52. These include the "Intermezzo," "Rondo," and "Etude" from his ballet *The Prodigal Son,* the "Scherzino" and "Scherzo" from the *Sinfonietta* in A, and the "Andante" from the first *String Quartet.*

Of the three transcriptions from *The Prodigal Son,* the first two may be recommended as concert pieces, while the third would be quite suitable for an intermediate student.

The transcription of the "Intermezzo," Opus 52 #1 (Figure 3.108), begins with an "Andantino" introduction, then immediately launches into a virtuosic "Presto" section that is dominated by fast eighth notes, especially staccato thirds. Only occasionally is the "Presto" tempo interrupted by slower waltz-like themes, although at the very end the material of the slow introduction has the final word.

Figure 3.108. Prokofiev, Opus 52 #1, transcription of the "Intermezzo" from *The Prodigal Son,* measures 1-4.
Figures 3.108. through 3.113., from Opus 52, reprinted by permission of Boosey and Hawkes, Inc.

The transcription of the "Rondo," Opus 52 #2 (Figure 3.109), dedicated to Artur Rubinstein, contains many difficult passages, despite its moderate tempo. In this charming transcription, Prokofiev keeps the performer occupied with plenty of leaps, changes of register and upbeat flourishes comprised of scales, arpeggios, or glissandi.

Figure 3.109. Prokofiev, Opus 52 #2, transcription of the "Rondo" from *The Prodigal Son,* measures 1-4.

The "Etude" from *The Prodigal Son* is an energetic perpetual-motion tarantella, centered in the mode of D dorian but featuring wide-ranging modulations and a coda that plays the D-major triad against the D-minor triad. Prokofiev's transcription of this etude, Opus 52 #3 (Figure 3.110), lies quite comfortably under the hand and would make a suitable choice for an intermediate student's repertoire. In introducing this piece, the teacher might spark the student's interest by explaining how Prokofiev's return to Russia after disappointments and poverty in the West parallels the Biblical story of the prodigal son.

Figure 3.110. Prokofiev, Opus 52 #3, transcription of the "Etude" from *The Prodigal Son,* measures 1-4.

The "Scherzino" from the *Sinfonietta* in A Major is a neo-Classical serenade with a theme that falls mainly into three-measure phrases. Prokofiev's transcription of the "Scherzino," Opus 52 #4 (Figure 3.111), lies moderately well under the hand, despite some awkward changes of hand position. The transcription could serve for an advanced student as a study in voicing, balance, and left-hand leaps.

Figure 3.111. Prokofiev, Opus 52 #4, transcription of the "Scherzino" from the *Sinfonietta* in A Major, measures 1-3.

The "Andante" from the first *String Quartet* contains some broad lyrical melodies and strong rhetorical climaxes. Prokofiev's transcription of this work, Opus 52 #4 (Figure 3.112) belongs in the category of a study score; it appears that, in an attempt to reproduce the string counterpoint, the composer has been forced to rely upon complex textures, awkward leaps, large stretches, arpeggiation of chords, and division of melodies between the hands.

Figure 3.112. Prokofiev, Opus 52 #5, transcription of the "Andante" from the first *String Quartet*, measures 1-2.

The "Scherzo" from the *Sinfonietta* displays, particularly in its theme, the rhythmic drive and precision of the young Prokofiev at his most robust. Prokofiev dedicated his transcription of this scherzo, Opus 52 #6 (Figure 3.113), to Vladimir Horowitz. This highly pianistic transcription could certainly be recommended for an advanced-intermediate student.

Figure 3.113. Prokofiev, Opus 52 #6, transcription of the "Scherzo" from the *Sinfonietta*, measures 1-2.

Opus 67, transcription of Peter and the Wolf

Peter and the Wolf, a work that has been used to introduce countless numbers of children to the orchestra, remains the one work of Prokofiev that is most widely known and loved by the general public. Prokofiev's piano transcription of *Peter and the Wolf,* Opus 67 (Figure 3.114), bears the same opus number as the orchestral version, and includes a narration written by the composer. This transcription could prove useful as a study or rehearsal score, or perhaps as an educational tool.

Figure 3.114. Prokofiev, Opus 67, transcription of *Peter and the Wolf,*
measures 2-3. Reprinted by permission of Boosey and Hawkes, Inc.

Opus 75, Ten Pieces from Romeo and Juliet

Prokofiev's Opus 75 consists of ten pieces transcribed from his ballet *Romeo and Juliet.* Despite the fact that the Bolshoi originally found Prokofiev's music unsuitable for dancing, *Romeo and Juliet* has taken its place as Prokofiev's most famous ballet, and has established him as one of Tschaikovsky's greatest heirs in this genre.

Prokofiev chose to transcribe as the first piece of Opus 75 the "Folk Dance" from *Romeo and Juliet* (Figure 3.115). An "Allegro giocoso" in 6/8 meter, this piece occasionally shows an affinity with the first movement of the seventh piano *Sonata.* Technically, the performer is given much broken-chord work, sometimes spaced à la Scriabin. There are also sustained tones that call for judicious use of the sostenuto and damper pedals. Despite its thematic repetitiveness, this transcription could still be recommended as a concert piece.

Figure 3.115. Prokofiev, Opus 75 #1, transcription of "Folk Dance"
from *Romeo and Juliet,* measures 3-6.
Figures 3.115. through 3.124., from Opus 75, used with the permission of G. Schirmer, Inc.,
New York (ASCAP) on behalf of RAIS (Russia).

The short "Scene," features a main theme that comes perilously close to the kind of music written as exercises for the ballet *barre*. However, Prokofiev enriches this simple theme through harmonic and melodic twists, irregular phrasings, and surprise modulations to distant keys. Like many of the works from Prokofiev's Soviet period, this piece reflects the composer's search for "a new simplicity" based upon melody that is "simple and comprehensible, without being repetitive or trivial" together with a technique and idiom that is "clear and simple, but not banal."[73] Prokofiev's transcription of this "Scene," Opus 75 #2 (Figure 3.116) could work as a concert piece for a skilled intermediate student with quick reflexes.

Figure 3.116. Prokofiev, Opus 75 #2, transcription of "Scene"
from *Romeo and Juliet,* measures 12-16.

The "Arrival of the Guests," styled as a polonaise in a moderate 3/4 meter, succeeds in presenting some strongly differentiated pompous and lyrical themes. Prokofiev's transcription of the "Arrival of the Guests," Opus 75 #3 (Figure 3.117), seems to strain to approximate orchestral spacings, but could still serve as a concert piece.

Figure 3.117. Prokofiev, Opus 75 #3, transcription of "Arrival of the Guests" from *Romeo and Juliet,* measures 1-2.

"Young Juliet" displays Prokofiev's sensitivity to the impetuous and lyrical moods of Shakespeare's heroine. The composer's transcription of this piece, Opus 75 #4 (Figure 3.118), employs broken triads pianistically, but suffers in places from thinness of sonority.

Figure 3.118. Prokofiev, Opus 75 #4, transcription of "Young Juliet" from *Romeo and Juliet,* measures 1-2.

Prokofiev gave "Masks" the unusual marking "Andante marziale." His somewhat impractical piano transcription of "Masks," Opus 75 #5 (Figure 3.119), could probably be most effectively performed by a virtuoso with large hands.

Figure 3.119. Prokofiev, Opus 75 #5, transcription of "Masks" from *Romeo and Juliet,* measures 5-6.

"The Montagues and the Capulets," a pesante march, has gained some popularity in its piano version because of its rugged, triadically based opening theme that contrasts with a lyrical trio derived from a theme associated with Juliet. Prokofiev's transcription of this piece, Opus 75 #6 (Figure 3.120), is highly pianistic, except possibly for some awkward arpeggiated chords in the trio.

Figure 3.120. Prokofiev, Opus 75 #6, transcription of "The Montagues and the Capulets" from *Romeo and Juliet,* measures 1, 3-4.

In "Friar Laurence," another musical portrait, Prokofiev gives this wise old Shakespearean character a rather expansive lyrical melody that unfolds between two statements of a portato melody. This transcription of "Friar Laurence," Opus 75 #7 (Figure 3.121), is a study in balance and cantabile playing.

Figure 3.121. Prokofiev, Opus 75 #7, transcription of
"Friar Laurence" from *Romeo and Juliet,* measures 1-2.

Prokofiev's "Mercutio," like Shakespeare's character of the same name, bursts with energy and spirit. Prokofiev's transcription of this piece, Opus 75 #8 (Figure 3.122), contains a few measures that, like some Romantic pieces, ideally require three hands, though only scored for two.

Figure 3.122. Prokofiev, Opus 75 #8, transcription of "Mercutio" from
Romeo and Juliet, measures 1-2.

"Dance of the Girls with Lilies" resembles perhaps a very refined polka. As an intermediate-level piece, the composer's transcription of this dance, Opus 75 #9 (Figure 3.123), could be used to teach elegant rubato and phrasing.

Figure 3.123. Prokofiev, Opus 75 #9, transcription of "Dance of the Girls with Lilies" from *Romeo and Juliet*, measures 4-5.

The final piece of Opus 75, "Romeo Bids Juliet Farewell," contains many profoundly expressive, lyrical melodies that unfold in various slow tempos. In this piano transcription, Opus 75 #10 (Figure 3.124), however, a few of the figures still seem to call for their original orchestral instrumentation, especially the quiet, rapidly repeated triads that are ideally suited for three flutes.

Figure 3.124. Prokofiev, Opus 75 #10, transcription of "Romeo Bids Juliet Farewell" from *Romeo and Juliet*, measures 1-3.

Opus 77-bis, transcription of "Gavotte" from Hamlet

Prokofiev's transcription of the "Gavotte" from *Hamlet*, Opus 77-bis (Figure 3.125), has much to recommend it as an advanced-intermediate-level piece. Its strengths include a robust introduction, an opening theme with some witty harmonic excursions, a more lyrical theme over a march-like bass, and frequent contrasts of articulation, texture, and dynamics. Technically, there are some fairly easy yet showy leaps and hand-crossings.

Figure 3.125. Prokofiev, Opus 77-bis, transcription of "Gavotte" from *Hamlet*, measures 4-6. Reprinted by permission of Boosey and Hawkes, Inc.

Opus 95, Three Pieces for Piano from Cinderella

Between 1942 and 1944, Prokofiev published a total of nineteen transcriptions for piano from his ballet *Cinderella*. Of these, three appeared as Opus 95, ten as Opus 97, and six as Opus 102.

The *Three Pieces for Piano from Cinderella*, Opus 95, take their titles from the dances on which they are based, i.e., "Pavane," "Gavotte," and "Slow Waltz." Generally, in *Cinderella*, Prokofiev tended to include more traditional dances or set-numbers than he did in *Romeo and Juliet*.

Prokofiev's transcription of the "Pavane," Opus 95 #1 (Figure 3.126), is marked by complexity of rhythm and texture, although in performance its virtuosic difficulties should be subsumed within the pulsations of the dance.

Figure 3.126. Prokofiev, Opus 95 #1, transcription of "Pavane" from *Cinderella*,
measures 1-2.
Figures 3.126. through 3.128., from Opus 95, used with the permission of
G. Schirmer, Inc., New York (ASCAP) on behalf of RAIS (Russia).

Prokofiev's transcription of the "Gavotte" from *Cinderella*,
Opus 95 #2 (Figure 3.127), leads from an incisive introduction into a
wryly humorous principal theme. As in the "Pavane," the player must
be able to execute quick leaps without disturbing the rhythm of the
dance.   Often in this gavotte, notes must be sustained by finger
substitution or via the damper or sostenuto pedal. This transcription
could possibly be assigned to an intermediate student as an
introduction to the sostenuto pedal.

Figure 3.127. Prokofiev, Opus 95 #2, transcription of "Gavotte" from *Cinderella*,
measures 1-2.

The transcription of the "Slow Waltz" from *Cinderella,* Opus 95 #3 (Figure 3.128), features complex rhythms, textures, and chromatic harmonies juxtaposed against a simple "oom-pah-pah" bass figure on the tonic chord, a figure that recurs at several structural points within the piece, perhaps as a signpost for the dancers. The leaps, arpeggiated chords, and counterpoint in this piece fortunately are made less formidable by the slowness of the tempo.

Figure 3.128. Prokofiev, Opus 95 #3, transcription of "Slow Waltz" from *Cinderella,* measures 3-5.

Opus 97, Ten Pieces for Piano from Cinderella

Of the *Ten Pieces for Piano from Cinderella,* Opus 97, only a few take their titles from dance forms. The ten titles are "Spring Fairy," "Summer Fairy," "Autumn Fairy," "Winter Fairy," "Grasshoppers and Dragonflies," "Orientale," "Passepied," "Capriccio," "Bourrée," and "Adagio."

Like the ten fairies in Tschaikovsky's *Sleeping Beauty,* the four fairies in Prokofiev's *Cinderella* are characterized through contrasting music.

For the dance of the "Spring Fairy," transcribed as Opus 97 #1 (Figure 3.129), Prokofiev has written a very fast scherzo in 6/8 with both hands frequently placed in the treble clef range. The fast 6/8 motion is temporarily interrupted by a quiet episode in 2/4 that calls for some easy hand-crossing.

Figure 3.129. Prokofiev, Opus 97 #1, transcription of "Spring Fairy"
from *Cinderella,* measures 1-2.
Figures 3.129. through 3.138., from Opus 97, used with the permission of
G. Schirmer, Inc., New York (ASCAP) on behalf of RAIS (Russia).

The dance of the "Summer Fairy" is marked "sognando"
(dreaming), a marking Prokofiev also used for the slow movement of
the eighth *Sonata.* Technically, Prokofiev's transcription, Opus 97 #2
(Figure 3.130), makes notable use of wide-ranging melodic arpeggios
and rapid pianissimo scale patterns.

Figure 3.130. Prokofiev, Opus 97 #2, transcription of "Summer Fairy"
from *Cinderella,* measures 1-2.

The chromatic figurations and rapid crescendi and diminuendi in the dance of the "Autumn Fairy," Opus 97 #3 (Figure 3.131), suggest pictorial associations with the howling of autumn winds.

Figure 3.131. Prokofiev, Opus 97 #3, transcription of "Autumn Fairy" from *Cinderella*, measures 1-2.

The music of the "Winter Fairy," transcribed as Opus 97 #4 (Figure 3.132), relies upon themes that ascend and descend within a narrow range, perhaps in an effort to suggest the stillness of a winter landscape.

Figure 3.132. Prokofiev, Opus 97 #4, transcription of "Winter Fairy" from *Cinderella*, measures 1-2.

The music of the four fairies from *Cinderella* could be classified as intermediate-level, except for the rapid flourishes in the second and third pieces. These difficulties could be mastered, perhaps, by an advanced-intermediate student.

"Grasshoppers and Dragonflies" from *Cinderella*, Opus 97 #5 (Figure 3.133), like "Parade of the Grasshoppers" from the *Music for Children*, leaps about humorously. With the exception of two rapid arpeggios, this piece should lie technically within the range of an advanced-intermediate student.

Figure 3.133. Prokofiev, Opus 97 #5, transcription of
"Grasshoppers and Dragonflies" from *Cinderella*, measures 1-2.

Prokofiev's transcription of the "Orientale," Opus 97 #6 (Figure 3.134), lives up to its name by virtue of its quintal chord formations, melismatic melodies, and repeated chords that mimic tambourines. This piece would probably appeal to an advanced-intermediate student with a taste for exotic color.

Figure 3.134. Prokofiev, Opus 97 #6, transcription of "Orientale,"
from *Cinderella*, measures 1-2.

The "Passepied," Opus 97 #7 (Figure 3.135), another of Prokofiev's neo-Classical dance-pieces, demonstrates the composer's flair for subtle humor through harmonic substitution. Despite the frequent leaps in this piece from one register to another, it would probably appeal to an advanced-intermediate piano student.

Figure 3.135. Prokofiev, Opus 97 #7, transcription of "Passepied," from *Cinderella*, measures 1-2.

The eighth piece of Opus 97, the "Capriccio" from *Cinderella* (Figure 3.136), changes moods mercurially. This piano transcription could be enjoyed by an intermediate student as a study in capricious timing and dynamic contrasts.

Figure 3.136. Prokofiev, Opus 97 #8, transcription of "Capriccio," from *Cinderella*, measures 1-2.

Prokofiev's transcription of the "Bourrée" from *Cinderella,* Opus 97 #9 (Figure 3.137), begins with a strongly marked theme cast in five-measure phrases. There are several measures in this piece that require a stretch of a ninth, as well as one instance of an unarpeggiated stretch of a twelfth.

Figure 3.137. Prokofiev, Opus 97 #9, transcription of "Bourrée," from *Cinderella,* measures 1-2.

The "Adagio" from *Cinderella* functions in the ballet as a romantic *pas de deux* for Cinderella and her prince. The piano version, Opus 97 #10 (Figure 3.138), suffers somewhat from complicated and widespread textures that do not seem convincingly pianistic, but instead suggest a straining to approximate orchestral sonorities. As a slow waltz in 9/8, it invites comparison with the slow movement of the sixth *Sonata,* which seems considerably more pianistic.

Figure 3.138. Prokofiev, Opus 97 #10, transcription of "Adagio," from *Cinderella,* measures 1-3.

Opus 102, Six Pieces for Piano from Cinderella

In 1944, Prokofiev published six more transcriptions from his ballet *Cinderella,* namely, "Waltz," "Cinderella's Variation," "Quarrel," "Waltz," "Pas-de-châle," and "Amoroso." These transcriptions tend to be longer and more sectionalized than those of either Opus 95 or Opus 97.

The transcription of the "Waltz," Opus 102 #1 (Figure 3.139), relies obviously in its themes upon the melodic device of octave displacement. With the exception of a more difficult section marked "Meno mosso della prima volta," it remains within the level of difficulty of the easier Chopin waltzes. Near the end of this piece, there occurs an intriguing rhythmic displacement of the lowest bass chords from the downbeat to the third beat of the measure.

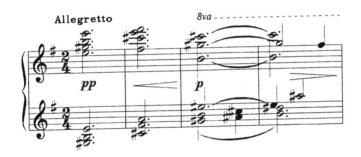

Figure 3.139. Prokofiev, Opus 102 #1, transcription of "Waltz," from *Cinderella,* measures 1-4.
Figures 3.139. through 3.144., from Opus 102, used with the permission of G. Schirmer, Inc., New York (ASCAP) on behalf of RAIS (Russia).

The title "Cinderella's Variation" uses the term "variation" in its balletic sense, meaning a solo piece for *danseur* or *danseuse,* in which the soloist is free to vary the choreography to his or her taste. The music of "Cinderella's Variation," transcribed as Opus 102 #2 (Figure 3.140), alternates between a theme in 2/4 meter and some contrasting waltz themes in 3/4 meter. In the waltz-like sections of the piano version, the right-hand part features jagged eighth-note melodic patterns, somewhat reminiscent of the figurations in Chopin's *Waltz* in G-flat, Opus 70 #2.

Figure 3.140. Prokofiev, Opus 102 #2, transcription of "Cinderella's Variation" from *Cinderella*, measures 1-3.

"Quarrel," transcribed for piano as Opus 102 #3 (Figure 3.141), appeals to the imagination through the use of sforzandi, incisive rhythms, offbeat chords, and sharp contrasts of register. In one section, Prokofiev introduces this convoluted pattern of syncopation:

Rhythmically, because of its four-against-three polyrhythms and complex syncopations, this piece would probably best suit an advanced student or artist.

Figure 3.141. Prokofiev, Opus 102 #3, transcription of "Quarrel"
from *Cinderella*, measures 1-2.

The "Waltz" in G minor, transcribed as Opus 102 #4
(Figure 3.142), has become one of Prokofiev's better-known pieces
from *Cinderella*. The thematic material of the "B" section,
particularly because of its octave displacements, shows a strong
resemblance to the themes of the "Waltz," Opus 102 #1. However, the
G-minor "Waltz" (Opus 102 #4) tends toward greater fullness of
texture. It also contains polyrhythms and a rather treacherous coda
that takes it well beyond the intermediate level.

Figure 3.142. Prokofiev, Opus 102 #4, transcription of "Waltz"
from *Cinderella*, measures 1, 4-6.

The next piece in this opus bears the French title
"Pas-de-châle," usually translated as "Dance with Shawls."
Prokofiev's transcription of the "Pas-de-châle" from *Cinderella*,

Opus 102 #5 (Figure 3.143) begins with a theme in moderate 4/4 meter, contrasting with more vigorous themes in 6/8 meter. This piece belongs technically in the advanced-level category.

Figure 3.143. Prokofiev, Opus 102 #5, transcription of "Pas-de-châle" from *Cinderella*, measures 4-6.

The transcription of the "Amoroso" from *Cinderella*, Opus 102 #6 (Figure 3.144), begins with some very lush Romantic harmonies. The "Amoroso" quality is further conveyed by the "dolcissimo" harp-like accompaniment of thirty-second notes present throughout the "Andante" middle section. The rather Lisztian climax gives the impression, however, that Prokofiev is perhaps attempting to reproduce an orchestral grandeur and sonority beyond the limits of the piano.

Figure 3.144. Prokofiev, Opus 102 #6, transcription of "Amoroso" from *Cinderella*, measures 1-4.

Opus 96, Three Pieces from War and Peace, and Lermontov

In between piano arrangements of pieces from *Cinderella*, Prokofiev published his Opus 96, transcriptions of three orchestral pieces, one from the opera *War and Peace* and two from the film *Lermontov*.

The "Waltz" from the opera *War and Peace*, Opus 96 #1 (Figure 3.145), changes key a remarkable number of times from sharps to flats and back again. Its length and difficulty place it among the advanced-level transcriptions.

Figure 3.145. Prokofiev, Opus 96 #1, transcription of "Waltz"
from *War and Peace*, measures 1-4.
Figures 3.145. through 3.147., from Opus 96, used with the permission of G. Schirmer, Inc.,
New York (ASCAP) on behalf of RAIS (Russia).

The "Contredanse" and "Mephisto Waltz" from *Lermontov* surely have the distinction of being among the very few pieces by a great composer to be arranged for piano from a film score.

In the "Contredanse" from *Lermontov*, Prokofiev revives a less common genre of eighteenth-century dance. Prokofiev's transcription of this "Contredanse," Opus 96 #2 (Figure 3.146), sparkles with staccato articulations and graceful slurs. In the middle section, a broken-octave figure in the left hand recalls an identical figure in the *Toccata,* Opus 11.

Moderato

Figure 3.146. Prokofiev, Opus 96 #2, transcription of "Contredanse"
from *Lermontov*, measures 1-3.

Prokofiev's "Mephisto Waltz" lacks the sensuousness or brilliance of its most famous Lisztian namesake and dwells instead upon the dark, ironic side of Mephistopheles's character. The piano transcription, Opus 96 #3 (Figure 3.147) features some very difficult passages, particularly the variation of the theme in measures 38-41.

Figure 3.147. Prokofiev, Opus 96 #3, transcription of "Mephisto Waltz"
from *Lermontov*, measures 4-7.

Transcriptions of Works by Other Composers

Prokofiev transcribed the *Organ Fugue* in D minor by Buxtehude in Bach-Busoni fashion. This transcription (Figure 3.148) calls for sixths in the right hand, octaves in the left hand, crescendi, diminuendi, ritardandi, and pervasive legato articulation. Such Romantic transcriptions have gone out of style as our knowledge of performance practice and the preference for performance of old music on original instruments has grown stronger. A piece like this Prokofiev transcription could, nevertheless, add novelty to a recital program.

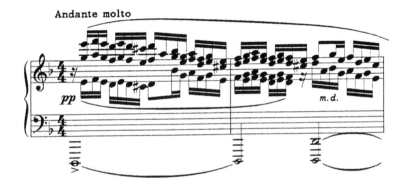

Figure 3.148. Buxtehude-Prokofiev, *Organ Fugue* in D minor, measures 1-2.
Reprinted by permission of Boosey and Hawkes, Inc.

Prokofiev's arrangement of Schubert *Waltzes* (Figure 3.149) rivals Liszt's *Soirées de Vienne* in its successful stringing together of several tuneful Schubert waltzes and Ländler into a coherent and engaging concert-piece. With its octaves, leaps, scales, and hand-crossings, it ranks among Prokofiev's more advanced transcriptions in difficulty.

Figure 3.149. Schubert-Prokofiev, *Waltzes,* measures 1-4.
Reprinted by permission of Boosey and Hawkes, Inc.

Chapter IV

CONCLUSIONS

Prokofiev was once asked to define a classical composer. He replied:

> A classical composer is a madman who writes music that his own generation dismisses as incomprehensible. This is because he has discovered a certain logic that is incomprehensible to them. Only in time does this logic become clear to all— usually after his death. If he had largely kept to rules laid down by past masters, he would have written music that all his contemporaries would have understood but it would have died with him. So he prefers to be thought mad and to have his work live after him.[74]

During the course of his life, Prokofiev went from being considered a musical revolutionary, to being considered a "classical composer," and even at times a musical reactionary. In his early piano compositions, he introduced many original techniques and helped to establish others as part of the mainstream of twentieth-century musical language. In these works, he also helped to adapt new aesthetic principles to piano music. In his second period, he came under the influence of Stravinsky and *Les Six,* producing works that tend to be less convincing than those in which he followed his personal creative instincts. In his third period, he returned to techniques and aesthetics established in his early piano works, producing works that, although conservative, include three of his masterpieces for piano: the sixth, seventh, and eighth *Sonatas.*

Prokofiev's musical innovations and his influence upon the course of twentieth-century music tend to be overlooked by historians because of his later conservatism. Ultimately, however, novelty becomes less important than musical quality in determining the place of a composer in history and the place occupied by that composer's works in the repertory.

Many of Prokofiev's works have entered the standard repertoires of artists and students and have achieved enduring popularity. Others, though less successful, retain considerable value for use as alternative teaching pieces or for variety in recital programming. The fact that a few of his piano works seem historically dated or weak in invention should not be surprising, however, in view of the quantity of Prokofiev's output and the fact that even Prokofiev himself had his personal favorites.

It is hoped that this book will have served to clarify Prokofiev's historical position as a composer of piano music and to encourage the reader to explore Prokofiev's piano works as a source for concert and teaching pieces. As a final word on the subject of Prokofiev's contribution to piano literature, a quote from Lawrence and Elizabeth Hanson deserves to be repeated; in their biography of Prokofiev, the Hansons state succinctly that "Prokofiev succeeded sufficiently well to ensure that piano writing will never be the same."[75]

END NOTES

Chapter One

1. Quoted in Abraham Chasins, *Speaking of Pianists* (New York: Alfred A. Knopf, 1957), p. 268.

2. Leonid Sabanieff, "Russia's Strong Man," *Modern Music* IV/2 (January-February, 1929), p. 6.

3. Serge Prokofiev, *Prokofiev by Prokofiev/A Composer's Memoir*, edited by David H. Appel, translated by Guy Daniels (Garden City, N.Y.: Doubleday, 1979), p. 176. (Subsequent references to this work will be listed by "Serge Prokofiev, autobiography" and page number only.)

4. Serge Prokofiev, autobiography, p. 299.

5. David Leslie Kinsey, "The Piano Sonatas of Serge Prokofiev: A Critical Study of the Elements of their Style," (Columbia University dissertation, 1959), p. 301. (Subsequent references to this work will be listed by author and page number only.)

6. David Leslie Kinsey, p. 265.

7. The term "socialist realism," which may have been coined by Stalin, refers to an aesthetic that satisfied Soviet bureaucratic tastes, typically through simplicity, optimism, nationalism, and glorification of life under the Communist regimes of the Union of Soviet Socialist Republics.

8. Nicholas Nabokov, *Old Friends and New Music* (Boston: Little, Brown, 1951), P. 144; quoted in David Gutman, *Prokofiev* (London: The Alderman Press, 1988), p. 84.

9. Donald Jay Grout, *A History of Western Music,* revised edition (New York: W. W. Norton, 1972), p. 704.

10. The term *"stile mécanique,"* as used in this book, has been borrowed from David Leslie Kinsey's dissertation on the subject of the piano sonatas of Serge Prokofiev. This term refers to a musical style whose aesthetic shows the influence of the machine. Prokofiev's interest in machine aesthetics is shown in several piano works, as well as works such as the second *Symphony* and the ballet *The Steel Step.*

11. The Futurist movement, founded in 1908 by F. T. Marinetti (1876-1944), soon attracted a highly talented group of Italian artists, including Umberto Boccioni (1882-1916), Giacomo Balla (1871-1958), Gino Severini (1883-1966), and Luigi Russolo (1885-1947). These artists sought to focus upon the dynamic aggressiveness of life in the twentieth-century city in the age of the machine. The futurists published several artistic manifestos, including "Futurist Painting: Technical Manifesto," (1910), and Luigi Russolo's "The Art of Noises" (1913).

12. Serge Prokofiev, autobiography, quoted in David Gutman, *Prokofiev,* p. 13.

13. Kinsey, p. 290.

14. Israel Vladimirovich Nestyev, *Prokofiev,* translated from the Russian by Florence Jones, with a foreword by Nicholas Slonimsky (Stanford: Stanford University Press, 1960), p. 465. (Subsequent references to this work will be listed by author and page number only.)

15. Quoted in Norman Demuth, *Musical Trends in the Twentieth Century,* (London: Rockcliff, 1952), p. 269. (Subsequent references to this work will be listed by author and page number only.)

Chapter Two

16. Patricia Ruth Ashley, "Prokofiev's Piano Music: Line, Chord, Key," (Rochester University dissertation, 1963), p. 37. (Subsequent references to this work will be listed by author and page number only.)

17. Serge Prokofiev, autobiography, p. 59.

18. Ashley, p. 41.

19. Nestyev, p. 269.

20. Quoted in Demuth, p. 269.

21. Ashley, p. 75.

22. Nestyev, p. 79.

23. Ashley, p. 73.

24. Ashley, p. 50.

25. Ashley, p. 75.

26. Quoted in Prokofiev, autobiography, p. 26.

27. Kinsey, pp. 249-250.

28. Ashley, p. 12.

29. Ashley, p. 42.

30. Ashley, p. 48.

31. Prokofiev, autobiography, p. 223.

32. Boris de Schloezer, "Serge Prokofiev," translated by David Leslie Kinsey, *La revue musicale* IX (July 1, 1921), p. 5; quoted in Kinsey, p. 259.

33. Prokofiev, interview with Olin Downes on February 4, 1930; quoted in David Ewen, *The Book of Modern Composers* (New York: Alfred A. Knopf, 1942), p. 143.

34. "Gary Graffman Plays Russian Piano Music," (Columbia ML-5844, 1963).

35. Kinsey, p. 294.

36. The group of French composers known as *Les six* was comprised of Georges Auric (1899-1983), Louis Durey (1888-1979), Arthur Honegger (1892-1955), Darius Milhaud (1892-1974), Francis Poulenc (1899-1963), and Germaine Tailleferre (1892-1983).

37. Kinsey, pp. 296-297.

38. Ashley, p. 202.

39. Lawrence and Elizabeth Hanson, *Prokofiev, the Prodigal Son/ An Introduction to his Life and Work in Three Movements* (London: Cassell, 1964), p. 155. (Subsequent references to this work will be listed by author and page number only.)

40. Ashley, p. 177.

41. Ashley, p. 195.

42. Ashley, p. 229.

43. Ashley, p. 235.

44. Ashley, p. 171.

45. Paul Cooper, *Perspectives in Music Theory*, second edition (New York: Harper & Row, 1981), p. 119.

46. Prokofiev married his first wife, the Spanish dancer Lina Llubera, in 1923. He brought her along when he returned to the Soviet Union in 1936, but several years later divorced her under a Soviet decree that dissolved marriages between Soviet citizens and foreigners. Prokofiev married his second wife, Mira Mendelson, in 1948, shortly before Lina Llubera-Prokofiev was arrested on charges of spying and sentenced to eight years in a Siberian labor camp.

47. Benjamin Suchoff, *Guide to the Mikrokosmos of Béla Bartók* (Silver Springs, Md.: Music Services Corp. of America, 1958), p. 12.

Chapter Three

48. Ashley, p. 70.

49. Nestyev, p. 20.

50. Ashley, p. 101.

51. Ashley, p. 110.

52. Ashley, p. 107.

53. Ashley, p. 114.

54. Ashley, p. 116.

55. Ashley, p. 124.

56. Quoted in Nestyev, pp. 52-53.

57. Ashley, p. 161.

58. Ashley, p. 208.

59. Ashley, p. 213.

60. Ashley, p. 221.

61. Quoted in Lawrence and Elizabeth Hanson, p. 49.

62. Ashley, p. 96.

63. Ashley, p. 82.

64. Nestyev, p. 31.

65. Ashley, p. 182.

66. Kinsey, p. 135.

67. Ashley, p. 290.

68. Harlow Robinson, *Serge Prokofiev* (New York: Viking Penguin, 1987), p. 431. (Subsequent references to this work will be listed by author and page number only).

69. Ashley, p. 303.

70. Ashley, p. 295.

71. Quoted in Robinson, pp. 130-131.

72. Nestyev, p. 176.

73. Prokofiev, article in *Izvestia* (November 16, 1934), quoted in Gutman, p. 109.

Chapter Four

74. Quoted in Hanson, p. 131.

75. Hanson, p. 65.

BIBLIOGRAPHY

Abraham, Gerald. *Eight Soviet Composers.* London: Oxford University Press, 1943.

Arnason, H. H. *History of Modern Art: Painting, Sculpture, Architecture.* New York: H. N. Abrams, 1968.

Ashley, Patricia Ruth. "Prokofiev's Piano Music: Line, Chord, Key." Rochester University Dissertation, 1963.

Austin, William W. "Aaron Copland." *New Grove Dictionary of Music and Musicians,* edited by Stanley Sadie. London: Macmillan, 1960.

Austin, William W. *Music in the Twentieth Century from Debussy through Stravinsky.* New York: W. W. Norton, 1966.

Bartók, Béla. *Improvisations.* New York: Boosey and Hawkes, 1939.

Bartók, Béla. *Out of Doors.* New York: Boosey and Hawkes, 1954.

Bartók, Béla. *Selected Works for the Piano.* New York: Schirmer, n.d.

Bartók, Béla. *Sonata.* Lynbrook, N.Y.: Boosey and Hawkes, 1939.

Beaumont, Anthony. *Busoni the Composer.* Bloomington: Indiana University Press, 1985.

Bennett, John Reginald. *Melodiya: A Soviet Russian L.P. Discography,* with a foreword by Boris Semeonoff and Anatoli Zhelezny. Westport, Connecticut: Greenwood Press, 1981.

Boucourechliev, Andre. "Olivier Messiaen." *New Grove Dictionary of Music and Musicians,* edited by Stanley Sadie. London: Macmillan, 1980.

Burge, David. *Twentieth-century Piano Music.* New York: Schirmer Books, 1990.

Busoni, Ferruccio. *An die Jugend: Giga, bolero e variazione; Studien nach Mozart.* Wiesbaden: Breitkopf and Härtel, n.d.

Busoni, Ferruccio. *An die Jugend: Introduzione e capriccio (Paganinesco).* Wiesbaden: Breitkopf and Härtel, n.d.

Busoni, Ferruccio. *An die Jugend: Preludio, fughetta, e fuga figuerta; Studien nach J. S. Bach's Wohltemperiertes Klavier.* Wiesbaden: Breitkopf and Härtel, n.d.

Busoni, Ferruccio. *An die Jugend: Preludio, fughetta, ed essercizio.* Wiesbaden: Breitkopf and Härtel, n.d.

Busoni, Ferruccio. *Elegien: 7 Klavierstucke.* Wiesbaden: Breitkopf and Härtel, n.d.

Cage, John. *Sonatas and Interludes for Prepared Piano.* New York: Henmar Press, 1960.

Calvacoressi, Michel D. *A Survey of Russian Music.* New York: Penguin Books, 1944.

Carter, Elliott. *Sonata.* New York: Mercury Music, 1948.

Chasins, Abraham. *Speaking of Pianists.* New York: Alfred A. Knopf, 1957.

Clough, Francis F., and G.J. Cuming. "Prokofiev on Records," *Tempo* XI (Spring, 1949): 32-34.

Clough, Francis F., and G.J. Cuming. *The World's Encyclopedia of Recorded Music.* Westport, Connecticut: Greenwood Press, 1970. (Reprint of London: Sidgwick and Jackson, 1966.)

Cooper, Martin, editor. *The Modern Age, 1890-1960,* Volume X of the *New Oxford History of Music,* edited by J. A. Westrup, et al. London: Oxford University Press, 1974.

Cooper, Paul. *Perspectives in Music Theory,* second edition. New York: Harper & Row, 1981.

Copland, Aaron. *Four Piano Blues.* New York: Boosey and Hawkes, 1949.

Copland, Aaron. *Piano Variations.* New York: Boosey and Hawkes, 1959.

Daniel, Oliver. "Ernst Krenek." *New Grove Dictionary of Music and Musicians,* edited by Stanley Sadie. London: Macmillan, 1980.

Debussy, Claude. *Children's Corner.* Paris: Durand, 1908.

Debussy, Claude. *Etudes.* Amsterdam: Broekmans & van Poppel, 1969.

Debussy, Claude. *Images, Book II.* Paris: Durand, 1907.

Debussy, Claude. *Piano Music (1888-1905),* second edition, corrected by Beveridge Webster. New York: Dover, 1972.

Debussy, Claude. *Preludes, Book I.* Paris: Durand, 1910.

Debussy, Claude. *Preludes, Book II.* Paris: Durand, 1913.

Demuth, Norman. *Musical Trends in the Twentieth Century.* London: Rockcliff, 1952.

Duo-Art Piano Music/A Classified Catalog of Music Recorded for the Duo-Art Reproducing Piano. New York: The Aeolian Company, 1927.

Eckstein, Maxwell, editor. *My Favorite Repertoire Album.* New York: Carl Fischer, 1948.

Frankenstein, Alfred. "Prokofiev on Microgroove," *High Fidelity* VI/3, (March, 1956): 95-104.

Friskin, James and Irwin Freundlich. *Music for the Piano.* New York: Rinehart, 1954.

"Gary Graffman Plays Russian Piano Music," produced by Paul Myers. Columbia ML 5844, 1963.

Gershwin, George. *Preludes.* New York: New World Music Corp., 1927.

Greenfield, Edward; Robert Layton; and Ivan Marsh; edited by Ivan Marsh. *The Penguin Guide to Compact Discs.* London: Penguin, 1990.

Griffiths, Paul. "Anton Webern." *New Grove Dictionary of Music and Musicians,* edited by Stanley Sadie. London: Macmillan, 1980.

Griffiths, Paul. *Bartók.* London: J. M. Dent, 1984.

Gutman, David. *Prokofiev.* London: The Alderman Press, 1988.

Hall, David. *The Record Book.* New York: Oliver Durrell, 1948.

Hanson, Lawrence and Elizabeth. *Prokofiev, the Prodigal Son/An Introduction to his Life and Works in Three Movements.* London: Cassell, 1964.

Hindemith, Paul. *Suite für Klavier, 1922.* London: Schott; New York: Associated Music Publishers, 1928.

Hindemith, Paul. *Tanzstücke, Opus 19.* Mainz: B. Schott's Söhne; New York: Associated Music Publishers, 1928.

Hinson, Maurice. *Guide to the Pianist's Repertoire,* 2nd rev. ed. Bloomington: Indiana University Press, 1987.

Hofmann, Michel Rostislav. *Serge Prokofiev/L'homme et son oeuvre.* Vol. 2 in *Musiciens de tous les temps.* Paris: Seghers, 1963.

Hopkins, G. W. "Maurice Ravel." *New Grove Dictionary of Music and Musicians,* edited by Stanley Sadie. London: Macmillan, 1980.

Ives, Charles. *Piano Sonata #2 ("Concord, Mass., 1840-60").* New York: Kalmus, 1968.

Kinsey, David Leslie. "The Piano Sonatas of Serge Prokofiev: A Critical Study of the Elements of Their Style." Columbia University dissertation, 1969.

Kirchner, Leon. *Sonata.* Long Island City, N.Y.: Bomart, 1950.

Kirkpatrick, John. "Charles E. Ives." *New Grove Dictionary of Music and Musicians,* edited by Stanley Sadie. London: Macmillan, 1980.

Krenek, Ernst. *Sonata #2,* Opus 59. Vienna: Universal, 1928.

Krenek, Ernst. *Sonata #4,* Opus 114. Long Island City, N.Y.: Bomart, 1950.

Lampert, Vera and Laszlo Somfai. "Béla Bartók." *New Grove Dictionary of Music and Musicians,* edited by Stanley Sadie. London: Macmillan, 1980.

Lyons, James. Record jacket notes to "Serge Prokofiev: Sonatas for Piano," performed by Yury Boukoff, piano. Westminster XWN 18369-71, 1957.

McAllister, Rita. "Serge Prokofiev." *New Grove Dictionary of Music and Musicians,* edited by Stanley Sadie. London: Macmillan, 1980.

MacDonald, Calum, compiled. *Gramophone Classical Catalogue,* with an introduction by Edward Greenfield. London: David and Charles, 1979.

MacDonald, Hugh. "Alexander Skryabin." *New Grove Dictionary of Music and Musicians,* edited by Stanley Sadie. London: Macmillan, 1980.

Merrick, Frank. "Prokofiev's Piano Sonatas, 1-5," *Musical Times* LXXVI, 1945.

Merrick, Frank. "Prokofiev's Works for Piano Solo," *Tempo* XI (Spring, 1949): pp. 26-29.

Messiaen, Olivier. *Etudes de rhythme,* 4 vols. Vol. I, *Ile de feu, 1;* Vol. II, *Ile de feu, 2;* Vol. III, *Neumes rhythmiques;* Vol. IV, *Modes de valeurs et d'intensités.* Paris: Durand; Philadelphia: Elkan-Vogel, 1947.

Messiaen, Olivier. *Technique of My Musical Language,* translated by John Satterfield. Paris: A. Leduc, 1956.

Messiaen, Olivier. *Vingt regards sur l'Enfant-Jésus.* Paris: Durand; Philadelphia: Elkan-Vogel, 1947.

Myers, Kurtz, ed. *Index to Record Reviews,* Vol. 2, based on material originally published in "Notes," the quarterly journal of the Music Library Association, between 1949 and 1977. Boston: G. K. Hall, 1978.

Neighbour, O. W. "Arnold Schoenberg." *New Grove Dictionary of Music and Musicians,* edited by Stanley Sadie. London: Macmillan, 1980.

Nestyev, Israel Vladimirovich. *Prokofiev,* translated from the Russian by Florence Jones, with a foreword by Nicholas Slonimsky. Stanford: Stanford University Press, 1960.

Nichols, Roger. "Francis Poulenc." *New Grove Dictionary of Music and Musicians,* edited by Stanley Sadie. London: Macmillan, 1980.

Northcott, Bryan. "Elliott Carter." *New Grove Dictionary of Music and Musicians,* edited by Stanley Sadie. London: Macmillan, 1980.

Poulenc, Francis. *Mouvements perpetuels,* revised ed. London: J. & W. Chester, 1939.

Poulenc, Francis. *Nocturnes.* Paris: Heugel, 1932.

Poulenc, Francis. *Novelettes.* London: J. & W. Chester, 1939.

Prokofiev, Serge Sergeevich. *Collected Works,* 30 Vols. Vols. I-XI, *Piano Solos.* Melville, N.Y.: Kalmus, n.d.

Prokofiev, Serge Sergeevich. *Deuxième sonatine, Opus 54 #2.* London: Boosey and Hawkes, 1947.

Prokofiev, Serge Sergeevich. *Divertimento,* Opus 43b. London: Boosey and Hawkes, n.d.

Prokofiev, Serge Sergeevich. *Four Grandmother's Tales, Op. 31; Four Pieces, Op. 32; Landscape, Op. 59.* New York: Edwin F. Kalmus, n.d.

Prokofiev, Serge Sergeevich. *Nine Sonatas for the Piano,* with a foreword by Paul Affelder. New York: International, 1971.

Prokofiev, Serge Sergeevich. *Peter and the Wolf,* Opus 67. New York: MCA, 1964.

Prokofiev, Serge Sergeevich. *Première sonatine, Opus 54 #1.* London: Boosey and Hawkes, 1947.

Prokofiev, Serge Sergeevich. *Prokofiev by Prokofiev: A Composer's Memoir,* edited by David H. Appel, translated by Guy Daniels. Garden City, N.Y.: Doubleday, 1979.

Prokofiev, Serge; Dmitri Kabalevsky; and Aram Khachaturian. *PKK: Serge Prokofieff, Dmitri Kabalevsky, and Aram Khachaturian/Their Greatest Piano Works*, with a foreword by Alexander Shealy. Carlstadt: Copa Publishing, 1972.

Ravel, Maurice. *An Album for Piano Solo: 1. Miroirs, 2. Sonatine, 3. Jeux d'eau.* Melville, N.Y.: Kalmus, n.d.

Ravel, Maurice. *Gaspard de la nuit.* Paris: Durand, 1908.

Ravel, Maurice. *Le tombeau de Couperin.* Paris: Durand, 1918.

Ravel, Maurice. *Valses nobles et sentimentales.* Paris: Durand, 1911.

Rezits, Joseph. *The Pianist's Resource Guide/Piano Music in Print and Literature on the Pianistic Art,* 8th ed. Park Ridge, Illinois: Pallma Music Corporation, 1974.

Robinson, Harlow. *Serge Prokofiev.* New York: Viking Penguin, 1987.

Roseberry, Eric. "Prokofiev's Piano Sonatas," *Music and Musicians* XXI/7 (1971), pp. 38-47.

Sabanieff, Leonid. *Modern Russian Composers,* translated by Judah A. Joffe. New York: International, 1927.

Sabanieff, Leonid. "Russia's Strong Man," *Modern Music* VI/1, January-February, 1929.

Sackville-West, Edward and Desmond Shawe-Taylor, with Andrew Porter and William Mann. *The Record Guide,* rev. ed. London: W.S. Cowell, 1955.

Salzman, Eric. Record jacket notes for "Prokofiev: The Complete Music for Solo Piano," performed by Gyorgy Sandor. Vox SVBX 5408-9.

Samuel, Claude. *Prokofiev,* translated by Miriam John. New York: Grossman, 1971.

Satie, Erik. *Piano Music,* volumes 1, 2, and 3. Paris: Edition Salabert, 1974.

Schoenberg, Arnold. Complete Works, edited by Josef Rufer, in cooperation with Richard Hoffmann, et al. Vol. 4, *Piano Works.* Mainz: B. Schott's Söhne, 1966.

Schonberg, Harold. *The Lives of the Great Composers,* revised edition. New York: W. W. Norton, 1981.

Scriabin, Alexander. *Selected Piano Works, Volume 1: Etudes,* edited by Gunter Philipp. Leipzig: Peters, 1966.

Scriabin, Alexander. *Selected Piano Works, Volume 3: Preludes, Poèmes, and other Pieces,* edited by Gunter Philipp. Leipzig: Peters, 1968.

Scriabin, Alexander. *Ten Piano Sonatas.* New York: MCA, 1949.

"Serge Prokofiev: *Cinderella, Sonata #2,* Sonatina pastorale," performed by Ramzi Yassa, piano. Pavane, ADW 7145, 1982.

"Serge Prokofiev," in *Bibliographic Guide to Music, 1987.* Boston: G. K. Hall, 1987.

"Serge Prokofiev," in *Bibliographic Guide to Music, 1989.* Boston: G. K. Hall, 1989.

"Serge Prokofiev," in *Bibliographic Guide to Music, 1992.* Boston: G. K. Hall, 1993.

"Serge Prokofiev," in *The Classical Catalogue,* No. 154 (Dec., 1992). Harrow, England: General Gramophone Publications, 1992.

"Serge Prokofiev," in *The Classical Catalogue,* No. 155 (June, 1993). Harrow, England: General Gramophone Publications, 1993.

"Serge Prokofiev," in *Koch International Classical Catalogue, 1992.* Westbury, N.Y.: Koch International, 1992.

"Serge Prokofiev," in *Long-Playing Record Catalog* [on microfilm]. Cambridge, Mass.: W. Schwann, 1949-1989.

"Serge Prokofiev," in *Phonolog Reports.* New York: Trade Service Corporation, 1991.

"Serge Prokofiev," in *Schwann CD.* Boston: W. Schwann, 1989.

"Serge Prokofiev," in [Schwann] *Opus,* Vol. 2 #2 (Spring 1991). Sante Fe, NM: Stereophile, 1991.

"Serge Prokofiev," in [Schwann] *Opus,* Vol. 3 #1 (Winter 1991-92). Sante Fe, NM: Stereophile, 1992.

"Serge Prokofiev," in *Schwann Opus,* Vol. 4 #2 (Spring, 1993). Santa Fe, NM: Stereophile, 1993.

Seroff, Victor. *Sergei Prokofiev/A Soviet Tragedy.* New York: Funk & Wagnalls, 1968.

Shostakovich, Dmitri. *Three Fantastic Dances,* Opus 1. New York: Edwin F. Kalmus, n.d.

Shostakovich, Dmitri. *Twenty-four Preludes and Fugues,* Opus 87. New York: Leeds, 1955.

Smith, Charles Davis. *Duo-Art Piano Music/A Classified Catalog of Music Recorded for the Duo-Art Reproducing Piano.* Monrovia, California: The Player Shop, 1987.

Stravinsky, Igor. *Serenade.* Berlin: Edition russe de musique, 1926.

Stravinsky, Igor. *Sonata.* London: Boosey and Hawkes, 1980.

Stravinsky, Igor. *Ten Short Piano Pieces,* edited by Soulima Stravinsky. London: Boosey and Hawkes, 1977.

Suchoff, Benjamin.   *Guide to the Mikrokosmos of Béla Bartók.* Silver Springs, Md.: Music Service Corporation of America, 1958.

Villa-Lobos, Heitor. *Prole do Bébé (The Baby's Family).* New York: E.B. Marks, 1946.

White, Eric Walter and Jeremy Noble. "Igor Stravinsky." *New Grove Dictionary of Music and Musicians,* edited by Stanley Sadie. London: Macmillan, 1980.

Wirth, Helmut. "Ferruccio Busoni." *New Grove Dictionary of Music and Musicians,* edited by Stanley Sadie.   London: Macmillan, 1980.

SCORES OF PROKOFIEV'S PIANO MUSIC

Collections

Album. Op. 2 #3; Op. 11; Op. 12 #1; Op. 17; Op. 22; Op. 54 #2; Op. 59 #3. Kalmus #03774. Melville, N.Y.: Kalmus, n.d.

Album of Prokofieff Masterpieces. Op. 2 #4; Op. 3 #1; Op. 4 #4; Op. 12 #1, 2, & 7; Op. 17 #3 & 5; transcriptions: Op. 25 (2nd & 3rd mvts.), Op.33-ter, Op. 52 #6, Op. 67 ("Triumphal March"), Op. 75 #2. New York: E.B. Marks, n.d.

Collected Works, 30 Vols. Vols. 1-11, *Piano Solos.* Melville, N.Y.: Kalmus, n.d.

      Vol. 1.   Op. 2, Op. 3, Op. 4, Op. 11
      Vol. 2.   Op. 12, Op. 17
      Vol. 3.   Op. 22, Op. 31, Op. 32, Op. 59 #2 & 3, Op. 65
      Vol. 4.   Op. 1, Op. 14, Op. 28
      Vol. 5.   Op. 29, Op. 38, Op. 135
      Vol. 6.   Op. 82, Op. 83
      Vol. 7.   Op. 84, Op. 103
      Vol. 8.   Transcriptions: Op. 25, Op. 33-ter, Op. 52
      Vol. 9.   Transcriptions: Op. 75, Op. 77-bis
      Vol. 10. Transcriptions: Op. 95, Op. 97, Op. 102
      Vol. 11. Transcriptions: Op. 96; *Organ Fugue* (Buxtehude); *Waltzes* (Schubert)

Piano Music of New Russia. Contains Prokofiev's Opus 12 #1; Opus 17 #3; Opus 25 (3rd mvt.); "Scherzo" from Opus 33-ter; "Triumphal March" from Opus 67; Opus 75 #1, 2, & 8. New York: E.B. Marks, 1943.

PKK: Serge Prokofieff, Dmitri Kabalevsky, and Aram Khachaturian/ Their Greatest Piano Works, with a foreword by Alexander Shealy. Contains Prokofiev's Op. 2 #3; Op. 3 #1, 2, & 4; Op. 4 #4; Op. 11; Op. 25 (3rd mvt.); Op. 33-ter; Op. 59 #2 & 3; Op. 62 #2 & 3; Op. 65 #1 & 4; Op. 67 ("Triumphal March"); Op. 96 #3; Op. 102 #4. Carlstadt: Copa Publishing, 1972.

Prokofiev/His Greatest Piano Solos.
   Op. 2 #4; Op. 3 #3; Op. 12 #1-10; Op. 22 #1; Op. 25 (3rd mvt.);
   Op. 52 #3;   Op. 65 #1-3, #5-12;   Op. 75 #2, 4, 6, 7, & 9;
   Op. 77-bis;   Op. 95 #2 & 3;   Op. 96 #2 & 3;   Op. 97 #1;
   Op. 102 #4; Op. 120 #1 & 2; Op. 122. Carlstadt: Ashley, 1979.

Selected Works, edited by Erno Balogh. Op. 2 #3 & 4 ; Op. 3; Op. 4 #4;
   Op. 11; Op. 12 #1 & 7; Op. 25 (3rd mvt.); Op. 33-ter; Op. 45B;
   Op. 52 #4 & 6; Op. 54 #2; Op. 59 #2 & 3; Op. 62; Op. 77-bis;
   Op. 96 #2 & 3. New York: G. Schirmer, n.d.

Selected Works, edited by Murray Baylor.   Op. 4 #4; Op. 11;
   Op. 12 #7; Op. 17; Op. 25 (3rd mvt.); Op. 28; Op. 31;
   Op. 33-ter; Op. 59 #3; Op. 75 #1-7. Van Nuys, Calif.: Alfred,
   1990.

Shorter Piano Works, edited by Dmitry Feofanov.   Reprinted from State Music Publishing House, Moscow, edition. Op. 2; Op. 3; Op. 4; Op. 11; Op. 12; Op. 17; Op. 22; Op. 31; Op. 32; Op. 45; Op. 54; Op. 59; Op. 62; Op. 65; and "Dumka." New York: Dover, 1992.

Six Pieces for Piano, edited by Serge Prokofiev.   Op. 2 #4; Op. 12 #1, 2, & 7; Op. 17 #3; Op. 22 #16.   New York: G. Schirmer, 1978.

Sonatas, edited by Gyorgy Sandor. New York: MCA, n.d.

Sonatas, edited by Irwin Freundlich. New York: Leeds, n.d.

Sonatas. Kalmus #03773. Melville, N.Y.: Kalmus, n.d.

Sonatas. Reprint of *Sonatas for Fortepiano* (Moscow: Izdatelatvo "Muzyka," 1967). New York: Dover, 1988.

Sonatas, 2 vols., with an introduction and performance notes by Peter Donohoe. London: Boosey and Hawkes, 1985.

Sonatas, with a foreword by Paul Affelder. New York: International, 1971.

Works, Piano, Selections. Includes Op. 64 #2; Op. 65 #6; Op. 96 #1 & 2; Op. 102 #2 & 3. Budapest: Editio Musica Budapest, 1979.

Individual Works (Listed by Opus Number)

Sonata #1, Opus 1
   AMP/Simrock (ed. Frey); International; Kalmus (K 3778); Leeds (ed. Cumpson); MCA (ed. Sandor); Peters (F 48); Rahter; Schauer (1102)

Four Etudes, Opus 2
   Forberg/Jurgenson; International; Kalmus (K 3788); MCA; Peters (F62-65)

Four Pieces, Opus 3
   Kalmus (K 3789); Rahter; Schauer (1103)

Four Pieces, Opus 4
   AMP/Simrock (ed. Frey, avail. separately); Boosey and Hawkes; International; Kalmus (K 3790); Leeds (ed. Foldes); MCA; Schauer (1104-1107)

"Diabolical Suggestion," Opus 4 #4
   EMB (Editio Musica Budapest)

Toccata, Opus 11
Forberg/Jurgenson; International; Kalmus (K 3791); MCA (ed. Sandor); Peters (F35)

Ten Pieces, Opus 12
AMP/Simrock (ed. Frey, avail. separately); International; Kalmus (K 3796); MCA (ed. Freundlich, 1960); Peters (F29); Schauer (3021-3030)

"March," Opus 12 #1
E.B. Marks; Forberg/Jurgenson; Schirmer (ed. Prokofiev)

"Gavotte," Opus 12 #2
E.B. Marks; Forberg/Jurgenson; Schirmer (ed. Prokofiev); Fischer (ed. Eckstein), in *My Favorite Repertoire Album,* 1948

"Rigaudon," Opus 12 #3
Forberg/Jurgenson

"Legend," Opus 12 #6
E.B. Marks

"Prelude," Opus 12 #7
Forberg/Jurgenson; MCA; Peters (F189); Schirmer

"Humoresque Scherzo," Opus 12 #9
Forberg/Jurgenson

"Scherzo," Opus 12 #10
Forberg/Jurgenson

Sonata #2, Opus 14
AMP/Simrock (ed. Frey); Forberg/Jurgenson; International; Kalmus (K 3779); Leeds (ed. Cumpson); MCA (ed. Sandor); Peters (F27); Schauer (1108)

Sarcasms, Opus 17
AMP/Simrock (ed. Frey); Boosey and Hawkes; E. B. Marks (ed. Benjamin); Forberg/Jurgenson; Kalmus (K 3797); MCA (ed. Freundlich); Schauer (1109)

Visions fugitives, Opus 22
Alfred (ed. Baylor, 1989); AMP/Simrock (ed. Frey);
Boosey and Hawkes (ed. Schneider, 1947); E.B. Marks (ed.
Benjamin); International (ed. Philipp); Kalmus (K 3798); MCA;
Schauer (1110); Schirmer (ed. Goldberger)

Classical Symphony, Opus 25
Boosey and Hawkes (PIB-345); Kalmus (K 3787)

"Gavotte," Opus 25 (3rd mvt.)
Boosey and Hawkes, Century (4086)

Sonata #3, Opus 28
AMP/Simrock (ed. Frey); Boosey and Hawkes (PIB-336);
International (ed. Philipp); Kalmus (K 3780); Leeds (ed.
Cumpson); MCA (ed. Sandor); Schauer (1111)

Sonata #4, Opus 29
Boosey and Hawkes; Kalmus (K 3781); Leeds (ed. Cumpson);
MCA (ed. Sandor)

Tales of the Old Grandmother, Opus 31
AMP; Boosey and Hawkes; International; MCA (ed. Foldes)

Tales of the Old Grandmother, Opus 31; *Four Pieces,* Opus 32;
and "Landscape," Opus 59 #1
Kalmus (K 3799)

Four Pieces, Opus 32
International (ed. Philipp); Leeds (ed. Sheldon); MCA

"Gavotte," Opus 32 #3
Boosey and Hawkes; Gutheil; International (ed. Philipp)

"Waltz," Opus 32 #4
Breitkopf & Härtel; Boosey and Hawkes

"March," from *Love for Three Oranges,* Opus 33-ter
Boosey and Hawkes (ed. Schneider); Century (4014);
E.B. Marks (ed. Sucra, 1936)

Sonata #5, Opus 38
  Boosey and Hawkes (PIB-337); International; Kalmus (3782);
  MCA (ed. Sandor)

Sonata #5, Opus 135 (rev. ed.)
  Kalmus

Divertissement, Opus 43B
  Boosey and Hawkes; MCA

Choses en soi, Opus 45 A & B
  Boosey and Hawkes; Kalmus

Six Transcriptions, Opus 52
  AMP (ed. Padwa, avail. separately);
  Boosey and Hawkes (avail. separately)

Two Sonatinas, Opus 54
  Boosey and Hawkes (avail. separately)

"Sonatinas," Opus 54 #2, 59 #3
  Kalmus (K 3800)

Three Pieces, Opus 59
  Boosey and Hawkes (avail. separately)

Pensées, Opus 62
  Boosey and Hawkes

Music for Children, Opus 65
  Alfred (ed. Palmer, 631); Boosey and Hawkes; International;
  Leeds/MCA (ed. Wolman); Ricordi; Schirmer (1772)

"Morning," Opus 65 #1
  Century (3796)

"Walk," Opus 65 #2
  Hansen (ed. Brimhall, #36120); MCA

"Tarantella," Opus 65 #4
   Century (3714); MCA (ed. Wolman)

"Waltz," Opus 65 #6
   MCA (ed. Wolman)

"March," Opus 65 #10
   MCA (ed. Wolman)

"Evening," Opus 65 #11
   MCA (ed. Wolman)

"Moonlit Meadows," Opus 65 #12
   MCA (ed. Wolman)

Peter and the Wolf, Opus 67
   Allans Music, Australia (707); Boosey and Hawkes (ed. Dunhill,
   PIB-325); MCA; Musicord (ed. Hirschberg); Peters (P 5730)

"Theme" from *Peter and the Wolf,* Opus 67
   Gordon V. Thompson, Canada

Ten Pieces from "Romeo and Juliet," Opus 75
   Leeds (ed. Fredericks); MCA; Peters (P 4790); Sikorski (2121)

"Gavotte" from *Hamlet,* Opus 77-bis
   Boosey and Hawkes; Kalmus (K 3801)

Sonata #6, Opus 82
   Boosey and Hawkes; Kalmus (K 3783); MCA (ed. Sandor);
   Peters (P 4788); Sikorski

Sonata #7, Opus 83
   Boosey and Hawkes; International (ed. Philipp); Kalmus
   (K 3784); Leeds (ed. Schmitz); MCA (ed. Sandor);
   Peters (P4745); Sikorski

Sonata #8, Opus 84
   Boosey and Hawkes; Kalmus (K 3785); Leeds (ed. Cumpson);
   MCA (ed. Sandor); Peters (P 4732); Sikorski

Three Pieces for Piano from "Cinderella," Opus 95
   Boosey and Hawkes; Kalmus; Leeds (ed. Cumpson);
   Peters (P 5769)

Three Pieces from "War and Peace" and "Lermontov," Opus 96
   Kalmus; Leeds (ed. Cumpson); MCA; Peters

Ten Pieces for Piano from "Cinderella," Opus 97
   Kalmus (K 3792); MCA (ed. Balogh); Peters (P 5769)

"Waltz," from *Cinderella,* Opus 102 #4
   Kalmus (K 3793); MCA; Peters (P 4774)

Sonata #9, Opus 103
   Boosey and Hawkes; Kalmus (K 3786); MCA (ed. Sandor);
   Peters (P 4769); Sikorski (2180)

Waltzes (Schubert-Prokofiev)
   Boosey and Hawkes; International

Organ Fugue in D minor (Buxtehude-Prokofiev)
   Boosey and Hawkes; Leeds

DISCOGRAPHY

RECORDINGS BY THE COMPOSER (Listed by Title)

"Composers Play Their Compositions."
   Includes performances by Serge Prokofiev of "Diabolical Suggestion," Opus 4 #4; "Scherzo," Opus 12 #10; *Sarcasms*, Opus 17 #1 & 2; *Tales of the Old Grandmother*, Opus 31 #2. Melodiya D010661-4.

"Eminent Bygone Pianists."
   Includes performance by S. Prokofiev of "Prelude," Opus 12 #7. Melodiya D11423-36.

"The Genius of Prokofiev and Busoni at the Piano."
   Contains performances by S. Prokofiev of "March," Opus 12 #1; "Rigaudon," Opus 12 #3; "Prelude," Opus 12 #7; "Scherzo," Opus 12 #10; "Intermezzo," from *Love for Three Oranges*, Opus 33-ter.
   Distinguished Recordings DR 102.

"Great Recordings of the Century." Serge Prokofiev, piano.
   Contains "Diabolical Suggestion," Opus 4 #4; *Visions fugitives*, Opus 22 #3, 5, 6, 9, 10, 11, 16, 17, 18; "Gavotte," Opus 25 (3rd mvt.); "Andante," from *Sonata #4*, Opus 29; *Tales of the Old Grandmother*, Opus 31 #2-3; "Gavotte," Opus 32 #3; "Etude," from *The Prodigal Son*, Opus 52 #3; "Landscape," Opus 59 #2; and "Sonatina pastorale," Opus 59 #3.
   HMV DB 5030-33; G.F JLP 5048; Angel COLH 34 (LP), 1958.

"Prokofiev Plays Prokofiev."
Contains "Diabolical Suggestion," Opus 4 #4; *Visions fugitives,* Opus 22 #3, 5, 6, 9, 10, 11, 16, 17, 18; "Gavotte," Opus 25 (3rd mvt.); "Andante," from *Sonata #4,* Opus 29; *Tales of the Old Grandmother,* Opus 31 #2 & 3; "Gavotte," Opus 32 #3; "Etude," from *The Prodigal Son,* Opus 52 #3; "Landscape" and "Sonatina pastorale," Opus 59 #2 & 3.
Pearl GEMM CD-9470 (CD), 1991.

"Serge Prokofiev Concert." [reproduced from phonorolls.]
Contains *Toccata,* Opus 11; "March," Opus 12 #1; "Gavotte," Opus 12 #2; "Rigaudon," Opus 12 #3; "Prelude," Opus 12 #7; "Scherzo," Opus 12 #10; *Sarcasms,* Opus 17 #1-2; *Tales of the Old Grandmother,* Opus 31 #3; "Intermezzo" from *Love for Three Oranges,* Opus 33-ter.
Everest X907 (LP), 1966.

RECORDINGS BY THE COMPOSER (Not Listed by Title)

"Diabolical Suggestion," Opus 4 #4; *Visions fugitives,* Opus 22 #3, 5, 6, 9, 11, 16, 17, 18; "Andante," from *Sonata #4,* Opus 29; *Tales of the Old Grandmother,* Opus 31 #2; "Etude" from *The Prodigal Son,* Opus 52 #3; "Landscape," Opus 59 #2; "Sonatina pastorale, Opus 59 #3.
Melodiya 5658/9.

Toccata, Opus 11; "March," Opus 12 #1; "Rigaudon," Opus 12 #3; "Scherzo," Opus 12 #10; *Sarcasms,* Opus 17 #1 & 2.
Melodiya 9887/8.

Toccata, Opus 11; "March," Opus 12 #1; "Gavotte," Opus 12 #2; "Rigaudon," Opus 12 #3; "Scherzo," Opus 12 #10; *Sarcasms,* Opus 17 #1 & 2; *Tales of the Old Grandmother,* Opus 31 #3.
Pye Ember GVC 40.

RECORDINGS BY THE COMPOSER (Piano Rolls)

Opus 11, *Toccata,* Duo-Art 6391(-3), 1921.

Opus 12, *Ten Pieces:*
  #1, "March." Duo-Art 6160(0), 1919; D-299; D-737.
  #2, "Gavotte." Duo-Art 6253(0), 1920.
  #3, "Rigaudon." Duo-Art 6344(0), 1920.
  #7, "Prelude." Duo-Art 6153(-3), 1919.
  #10, "Scherzo." Duo-Art 67440, 1924.

Opus 17, *Sarcasms:*
  #1 & 2. Duo-Art 6210(0), 1919; D-205.

Opus 31, *Tales of the Old Grandmother:*
  #3. Duo-Art 6826-3, 1924.

Opus 33-ter, "Intermezzo" from *Love for Three Oranges.*
  Duo-Art 6477(0), 1921.

Opus 33-ter, "March" from *Love for Three Oranges.*
  Duo-Art br 8018.

RECORDINGS BY OTHER ARTISTS

Complete Works

"Prokofiev: The Complete Works for Solo Piano," performed by
Boris Berman.
Vol. 1. *Four Pieces,* Opus 32; "March" and "Scherzo," from
Love for Three Oranges, Opus 33-ter; *Sonata #5,* Opus 38/135;
Ten Pieces from "Romeo and Juliet," Opus 75.
Chandos CHAN 8851 (CD), ABTD 1468 (Cassette), 1991.
Vol. 2. *Sarcasms,* Opus 17; *Visions fugitives,* Opus 22; *Tales of
the Old Grandmother,* Opus 31; *Sonata #7,* Opus 83.
Chandos CHAN 8881 (CD), ABTD 1494 (Cassette), 1991.
Vol. 3. *Sonata #4,* Opus 29; *Six Transcriptions,* Opus 52;
Music for Children, Opus 65.
Chandos CHAN 8926 (CD), ABTD 1527 (Cassette).
Vol. 4. *Four Pieces,* Opus 3; *Sonata #8,* Opus 84; *Ten Pieces
from "Cinderella,"* Opus 97.
Chandos CHAN 8976 (CD), ABTD 1565 (Cassette).
Vol. 5. *Sonata #1,* Opus 1; *Four Pieces,* Opus 4; *Two Sonatinas,*
Opus 54; *"Gavotte" from Hamlet,* Opus 77-bis; *Three Pieces
from "War and Peace" and "Lermontov,"* Opus 96; *Organ
Prelude and Fugue* (Buxtehude-Prokofiev).
Chandos CHAN 9017 (CD).
Vol. 6. *Ten Pieces,* Opus 12; *Sonata #3,* Opus 28; *Pensées,*
Opus 62; *Three Pieces from "Cinderella,"* Opus 95.
Chandos CHAN 9069 (CD)
Vol. 7. *Sonata #2,* Opus 14; *Three Pieces,* Opus 59;
Six Pieces from "Cinderella", Opus 102; *"Dumka"; Waltzes*
(Schubert-Prokofiev). Chandos CHAN 9119 (CD).
Vol. 8. *Four Etudes,* Opus 2; *Divertimento,* Opus 43-bis;
Choses en soi, Opus 45; *Sonata #9,* Opus 103.
Chandos CHAN 9211 (CD), 1994.
(Volume 9 to be released on the Chandos label.)

"Prokofiev: The Complete Works for Solo Piano," performed by
Gyorgy Sandor, with record jacket notes by Eric Salzman.
Vox SVBX 5408 and 5409 (Two 3-LP sets);
Vol. 1. - CDX3 3500 (Three CD's),
Vol. 2. - CDX2 5514 (Two CD's).

Complete Piano Sonatas

Complete piano sonatas, performed by Balageas.
Musical Heritage Society. MHS 3034-7 (4 LP's).

Complete piano sonatas, titled: "Serge Prokofiev: Sonatas for
Piano [#1-9]," performed by Yury Boukoff.
Westminster XWN 18369-71 (3 LP's), 1957.

Complete piano sonatas, performed by F. Chiu.
Harmonia Mundi 907086-88 (3 CD's).

Complete piano sonatas, titled: "Prokofiev/The Piano Sonatas,"
performed by John Lill.   Available as a complete set of
three CD's (ASV CDDCS 314), or as individual volumes:
Vol. 1.   *Sonatas #1-3; Visions fugitives,* Opus 22; *Sonatinas,*
Opus 54.
Academy Sound and Vision. ASV CDDCA 753 (CD),
ZCDCA 753 (Cassette), 1991.
Vol. 2.   *Sonatas #4-6;* "Sonatina pastorale," Opus 59 #3.
ASV CDDCA 754 (CD), ZCDCA 754 (Cassette), 1991.
Vol. 3.   *Sonatas #7-9.*
ASV CDDCA 755 (CD), ZCDCA 755 (Cassette), 1991.

Complete piano sonatas, performed by M. McLachlan.
Vol. 1.   *Sonatas #1,4,5,9,10.* Olympia OCD-255 (CD), 1990.
Vol. 2.   *Sonatas #2,7,8.* Olympia OCD-256 (CD), 1990.
Vol. 3.   *Sonatas #3,6.* Olympia OCD-257 (CD), 1990.

Complete piano sonatas, titled: "Sergei Prokofiev/Complete Piano
Sonatas," performed by Barbara Nissman.
Vol. 1.   *Sonatas #1-5* (including both versions of *Sonata #5).*
Newport Classics NCD 60092 (CD), NCC 60092 (Cassette),
1989.
Vol. 2.   *Sonatas #6-8.*
Newport Classics NCD 60093 (CD), 1989.
Vol. 3.   *Sonatas #9-10; Four Pieces,* Opus 4 #4; *Toccata,*
Opus 11; *Sarcasms,* Opus 17; *Visions fugitives,* Opus 22.
Newport Classics NCD 60094 (CD), NCC 60094 (Cassette),
1990.

Complete piano sonatas, performed by Nikolai Petrov.
Vol. 1. *Sonatas #2,4,6.* Melodiya SUCD 10-00207 (CD).
Vol. 2. *Sonatas #1,3,5,7.* Melodiya SUCD 10-00208 (CD).
Vol. 3. *Sonatas #8,9.* Melodiya SUCD 10-00209 (CD).

Complete piano sonatas, performed by Matti Raekillo.
Vol. 1. *Sonatas #1-3; Visions fugitives,* Opus 22.
Ondine ODE 729 (CD).
Vol. 2. *Sonatas #4, #5* (original version), *#6.*
Ondine ODE 761 (CD).
Vol. 3. *Sonatas #7,8,9.* Ondine ODE 716 (CD).

Other Collections (By Title)

"Early   Piano   Works,"   performed   by   B.   Vodenicharov.
Contains *Toccata,* Opus 11; *Sarcasms,* Opus 17; *Visions
fugitives,* Opus 22; *Tales of the Old Grandmother,* Opus 31;
Sonata #5, Opus 38.
Etcetera KTC 1122 (CD).

"First   Pieces   for   Piano,"   performed   by   A.   Rahman   El   Bacha.
"Allegretto in a," (1904-5); "Scherzo in D," (1904-5); *Sonata #1,*
Opus 1; *Four Etudes,* Opus 2; *Four Pieces,* Opus 3;
Four Pieces, Opus 4.
Forlane UCD 19596 (CD).

"Sviatoslav Richter at Carnegie Hall, Oct. 23, 1960," performed by
S. Richter, piano. Contains "Landscape," Opus 59 #2; "Sonatina
pastorale," Opus 59 #3; "Pensée," Opus 62 #3; *Sonata #6,*
Opus 82; *Sonata #8,* Opus 84; "Gavotte," from *Cinderella,*
Opus 95 #2.
Columbia M2L 282 (LP).

Collections and Individual Works (by Opus Number)

Opus 1, *Sonata #1*, performed by M. Béroff.
    EMI/Pathfinder 2C 069 73102 (LP), 1986.
Opus 1, *Sonata #1*, performed by R. Cornman.
    Decca FST 153515.
Opus 1, *Sonata #1*, performed by V. Kameníková.
    Supraphon 1111 3374.
Opus 1, *Sonata #1*, performed by S. Pertacarolli.
    Ermitage ERM 402 (CD).
Opus 1, *Sonata #1*, performed by J. Shin' Ar.
    Pick. MCD 67 (CD), 1991.

Opus 2, *Four Etudes:*
    #3, performed by E. Kissin.
    RCA RD60443 (CD), RK60443 (Cassette), 1990.
Opus 2, *Four Etudes:*
    #3, performed by N. Petrov.
    Melodiya D 023027/8 (LP).

Opus 3, *Four Pieces,* performed by A. Vedernikov.
    Melodiya D 017091/2 (LP).

Opus 4, *Four Pieces,* performed by I. Janssen.
    Globe GLO-5015 (CD), 1989.
Opus 4, *Four Pieces,* performed by T. Judd.
    DBR 3001, 1980.
Opus 4, *Four Pieces,* performed by B. Moiseiwitsch.
    Koch 37035-2 (CD), 1991.
Opus 4, *Four Pieces,* performed by A. Vedernikov.
    Melodiya D 107091/2 (LP).
Opus 4, *Four Pieces:*
    #3, "Despair" and #4, "Diabolical Suggestion,"
    performed by C. Biyo. Melodiya D 010359/60 (LP).
Opus 4, *Four Pieces:*
    #4, "Diabolical Suggestion," performed by S. Cherkassy.
    Vox 16025, 1947.

Opus 4, *Four Pieces:*
#4, "Diabolical Suggestion," performed by A. Gavrilov.
ASD 3600 (LP), 1978; EMI EG 290326-1, EG 290326-4, 1985.
Opus 4, *Four Pieces:*
#4, "Diabolical Suggestion," performed by V. Kamyshov.
Melodiya SM 02423/4.
Opus 4, *Four Pieces:*
#4, "Diabolical Suggestion," performed by B. Moiseiwitsch.
HMV E530, Victor 1449, 1929.
Opus 4, *Four Pieces:*
#4, "Diabolical Suggestion," performed by S. Prokofiev.
In Sync C-4148 (Cassette).
Opus 4, *Four Pieces:*
#4, "Diabolical Suggestion," performed by S. Richter.
Euro 206 402; Vanguard VRS 1102 (LP), 1963;
Memr 991002 (CD).
Opus 4, *Four Pieces:*
#4, "Diabolical Suggestion," performed by Artur Rubinstein.
Duo-Art 6922-4 (Piano Roll), 1925.
Opus 4, *Four Pieces:*
#4, "Diabolical Suggestion," performed by G. Tacchino.
Pierre Verany PV 791022 (CD), 1990.
Opus 4, *Four Pieces:*
#4, "Diabolical Suggestion," performed by S. Weissenberg.
Columbia ML 2099 (LP), 1950.
Opus 4, *Four Pieces:*
#4, "Diabolical Suggestion," performed by G. Werschenska.
HMV DA 5200, 1938.

Opus 11, *Toccata,* performed by M. Argerich.
DGG LPM 18672 (LP), 1961; DGG 2725 108;
DGG 3374 108, 1982; Nuov 6716-DM (CD).
Opus 11, *Toccata,* performed by L. Berman.
HUN HLX-90048-1 (LP); MTR MCS-2135 (LP).
Opus 11, *Toccata,* performed by Y. Boukoff.
Philips A76700 R.
Opus 11, *Toccata,* performed by S. Cherkassy.
Am. Vox, set 624, 1948.

Opus 11, *Toccata,* performed by S. François.
Columbia CX 1135, FCX 218, QCX 10087, ESBF 113;
Angel 35045 (LP).
Opus 11, *Toccata,* performed by V. Horowitz.
Victor 12-0428, 1948; RCA 60377-2-RG (CD),
RCA 60377-4-RG (Cassette), 1990; RCA GD 89789 (CD),
RCA GK 89789 (Cassette); Angel H-63538-C (CD).
Opus 11, *Toccata,* performed by I. Janssen.
Globe GLO-5015 (CD), 1989.
Opus 11, *Toccata,* performed by C. Katsaris.
TELD 642479, 442479, 1988.
Opus 11, *Toccata,* performed by R. Lewenthal.
Westminster WXN 18362 (LP), 1956.
Opus 11, *Toccata,* performed by T. Nikolayeva.
Melodiya D 6125/6 (LP).
Opus 11, *Toccata,* performed by R. Pöntinen.
Bis 276 (LP), 1985.
Opus 11, *Toccata,* performed by H. Roloff.
PV 36072.
Opus 11, *Toccata,* performed by L. Steuber.
Disc set 803, 1947.
Opus 11, *Toccata,* performed by T. Trotter.
Hyperion A66216, KA 66216.

Opus 12, *Ten Pieces,* performed by I. Janssen.
Globe GLO-5015 (CD), 1989.
Opus 12, *Ten Pieces,* performed by C. Katsaris.
TELD 642479, 442479, 1988.
Opus 12, *Ten Pieces,* performed by N. Petrov.
Melodiya SM 02807/8.
Opus 12, *Ten Pieces,* performed by A. Vedernikov.
Melodiya 017091/2 (LP).
Opus 12, *Ten Pieces:*
#1, "March"; and #2, "Gavotte," performed by L. Cassini.
Muza 1113.
Opus 12, *Ten Pieces:*
#2, "Gavotte," performed by M. Slezareva. USSR 22528.

Opus 12, *Ten Pieces:*
#2, "Gavotte"; #3, "Rigaudon"; #6, "Legend"; #7, "Prelude";
#8, "Allemande"; and #9, "Humoresque Scherzo," performed by
V. Sofronitsky. Melodiya D 9047/8 (LP), D 016161/2 (LP)

Opus 12, *Ten Pieces:*
#3, "Rigaudon," performed by P. Cooper. PC NH9.

Opus 12, *Ten Pieces:*
#6, "Legend," performed by S. Richter. Memr 991002 (CD).

Opus 12, *Ten Pieces:*
#6, "Legend"; #7, "Prelude"; and #9, "Humoresque Scherzo,"
performed by H. Graf.
Period 527, 599; Nixa PLP 527.

Opus 12, *Ten Pieces:*
#7, "Prelude," performed by A. Borofsky. Vic. 11-8741.

Opus 12, *Ten Pieces:*
#7, "Prelude," performed by Y. Boukoff.
Philips A76700 R.

Opus 12, *Ten Pieces:*
#7, "Prelude," performed by C. de Groot.
Philips N00632 R.

Opus 12, *Ten Pieces:*
#7, "Prelude," performed by Z. Drziewiecki.
Syrena 6565 (1930).

Opus 12, *Ten Pieces:*
#7, "Prelude," performed by E. Gilels. MACD 746 (CD).

Opus 12, *Ten Pieces:*
#7, "Prelude," performed by M. Kochinski. OLS 176.

Opus 12, *Ten Pieces:*
#7, "Prelude," performed by T. Nikolayeva.
Melodiya D 6125/6 (LP); Reli CR 911026 (CD).

Opus 12, *Ten Pieces:*
#7, "Prelude," performed by H. Roloff. PV 36072.

Opus 12, *Ten Pieces:*
#7, "Prelude," performed by O. Santoliquido.
Parlophone AT 0128.

Opus 12, *Ten Pieces:*
#7, "Prelude," performed by M.-A. Süss. Deno CO-76611 (CD).

Opus 12, *Ten Pieces:*
#7, performed by G. Tacchino.
Pierre Verany PV791022 (CD), 1990.

Opus 12, *Ten Pieces:*
    #7, "Prelude," performed by M. von Zadora.
    Polydor 23022, 1929.
Opus 12, *Ten Pieces:*
    #7, "Prelude," performed by M. Voskrensky.
    Melodiya D 5934/5 (LP), D 035279/80 (LP).

Opus 14, *Sonata #2,* performed by L. Berman.
    DG 253 095 (LP), DG 3301 095 (Cassette), 1979.
Opus 14, *Sonata #2,* performed by M. Béroff.
    EMI/Pathfinder 2C 069 73102 (LP), 1986.
Opus 14, *Sonata #2,* performed by Biret. Finnadar 125 (LP).
Opus 14, *Sonata #2,* performed by L. Cabasso. Valois V 4655 (CD).
Opus 14, *Sonata #2,* performed by R. Cornman. London LL 553 (LP).
Opus 14, *Sonata #2,* performed by B. Douglas.
    RCA 60779-2-RC (CD).
Opus 14, *Sonata #2,* performed by E. Gilels.
    Concert Hall CHS 1311 (LP); Chant du monde LDY 8121;
    Chant du monde LDC 278978 (CD); USSRM. D 492/3;
    Colosseum CRLP 186 (LP).
Opus 14, *Sonata #2,* performed by G. Graffman.
    Columbia ML 5844 (LP), 1963; ML 6444.
Opus 14, *Sonata #2,* performed by S. Henig. CBC SM 118, 1970.
Opus 14, *Sonata #2,* performed by I. Janssen.
    Globe GLO-5015 (CD), 1989.
Opus 14, *Sonata #2,* performed by T. Joselson. RCA ARL1-1570.
Opus 14, *Sonata #2,* performed by V. Kamyshov.
    Melodiya SM 02423/4.
Opus 14, *Sonata #2,* performed by V. Krainev.
    Newport Classics NCD 60112 (CD),
    Newport Classics NCC 60112 (Cassette), 1990;
    MCA Classics AED 68019 (CD), AEC 68019 (Cassette), 1990.
Opus 14, *Sonata #2,* performed by A. Moreira-Lima.
    Melodiya SM 03091/2.
Opus 14, *Sonata #2,* performed by N. Petrov.
    Melodiya SUCD 10-00207 (CD); Olympia OCD 280 (CD), 1991.
Opus 14, *Sonata #2,* performed by S. Richter.
    AS Disc AS340 (CD); Decca 436 451-2DH2 (CD), 1993;
    Nuova Era 2363 (CD), 1990; Praga PR 250 015 (CD);
    Rococo 2143.

Opus 14, *Sonata #2*, performed by N. Starkman.
Melodiya D 04378/9.
Opus 14, *Sonata #2*, performed by G. Tacchino.
Pierre Verany PV 791022 (CD), 1990.
Opus 14, *Sonata #2*, performed by S. Veselka.
Victoria VCD 19024 (CD).
Opus 14, *Sonata #2*, performed by D. Walsh.
Music and Arts CD 669-1 (CD).
Opus 14, *Sonata #2*, performed by R. Yassa.
Pavane ADW-7145 (LP), 1982; ADW-7199 (CD), 1990.

Opus 17, *Sarcasms*, performed by I. Khudoley.
Melodiya D 17643/4 (LP).
Opus 17, *Sarcasms*, performed by E. Novitskaya.
Melodiya/Angel SR-40164.
Opus 17, *Sarcasms*, performed by S. Scheja. Bis 155 (LP).
Opus 17, *Sarcasms*, performed by V. Sofronitsky.
Melodiya D 019641/2 (LP).
Opus 17, *Sarcasms*, performed by S. Veselka.
Victoria VCD 19024 (CD).
Opus 17, *Sarcasms*, performed by O. Volkov.
MCA Classics. AED-10155 (CD).
Opus 17, *Sarcasms*, performed by M. Zeltser.
Columbia MX 34564 (LP), 1978.
Opus 17, *Sarcasms:*
#1, performed by M.-A. Hamelin. DA COC D 379 (CD), 1991.
Opus 17, *Sarcasms:*
#3, 4, & 5, performed by E. Miansarov.
Melodiya D 04306/7 (LP).
Opus 17, *Sarcasms:*
#3, performed by V. Sofronitsky. Melodiya D 9047/8.
Opus 17, *Sarcasms:*
#5, performed by A. Borofsky.
Decca DE 7053; Polydor 561095, 1932; Vic. 10-1241, 1946.
Opus 17, *Sarcasms:*
#5, performed by V. Sofronitsky. Melodiya D 106257/8.

Opus 22, *Visions fugitives*, performed by M. Béroff.
EMI/Pathfinder 2C 069 73102 (LP), 1986;
EMI CMS7 62542-2; EMI Classics CDZB-62542 (CD).

Opus 22, *Visions fugitives,* performed by L. Cabasso.
Auvi V 4655 (CD).
Opus 22, *Visions fugitives,* performed by N. Demidenko.
Conifer CDCF 204 (CD); Conifer MCFC 204 (Cassette), 1991.
Opus 22, *Visions fugitives,* performed by M. Deyanova.
Nimbus NI-5176 (CD).
Opus 22, *Visions fugitives,* performed by E. Gilels. MACD 746 (CD).
Opus 22, *Visions fugitives,* performed by T. Joselson.
RCA ARL1-2158 (LP), 1977; ARS1-2158 (CD),
ARK1-2158 (Cassette).
Opus 22, *Visions fugitives,* performed by V. Kameníková.
Supraphon 1111 3374.
Opus 22, *Visions fugitives,* performed by D. Müller.
Nuova Era 7023 (CD).
Opus 22, *Visions fugitives,* performed by H. Neuhaus.
Monitor 2064.
Opus 22, *Visions fugitives,* performed by E. Novitskaya.
Melodiya/Angel S-40164.
Opus 22, Visions fugitives, performed by L. Pennario.
Capitol P8113.
Opus 22, *Visions fugitives,* performed by S. Richter.
AS Disc AS 334 (CD).
Opus 22, *Visions fugitives,* performed by D. Rubinstein.
Musical Heritage Society MHS-1794.
Opus 22, *Visions fugitives,* performed by G. Sandor.
TV 37066 S, 1975.
Opus 22, *Visions fugitives,* performed by P. Stepan.
SUA ST 50697, 1967.
Opus 22, *Visions fugitives* (selections), performed by
A. Borovsky. Victor 10-1241, 1946.
Opus 22, *Visions fugitives* (selections), performed by
Artur Rubinstein.
RCA 5670-2-RC (CD); RCA RD85670 (CD);
Ermitage ERM 108S (CD).
Opus 22, *Visions fugitives:*
#1-3, 6, 9-12, 14, 16, 18, performed by Artur Rubinstein.
RCA RL 42024.
Opus 22, *Visions fugitives:*
#1-3, 7, & 11, performed by V. Sofronitsky.
Melodiya D 013379/80 (LP).

Opus 22, *Visions fugitives:*
#1-4, 6, 7, 10, 12, 17, & 18, performed by V. Sofronitsky.
Melodiya D 019641/2 (LP).
Opus 22, *Visions fugitives:*
#1-4, 10, 14, 16, performed by S. Novikoff. BaM 90.
Opus 22, *Visions fugitives:*
#1, 3-6, 10, 11, 14, 16, & 17, performed by D. Bashkirov.
Melodiya D 08751/2 (LP), S 0237/8.
Opus 22, *Visions fugitives:*
#1, 3, 4, 6, 17, 18, performed by S. François.
CCX 1135, FCX 218, QCX 10087, Angel 35045.
Opus 22, *Visions fugitives:*
#1, 3, 5, 6, 10, 14, 15, 16, 17, & 18, performed by I. Graubin.
Melodiya D 024949/50 (LP).
Opus 22, *Visions fugitives:*
#1, 3, 5, 7, 8, 10, 11, & 17, performed by E. Gilels.
Columbia/Melodiya M-33824; Eurodisc 86 323.
Opus 22, *Visions fugitives:*
#3, 5, 9-11, 17, performed by E. Gilels.
Chant du monde LDA 8104;
Chant du monde LDC 278 979 (CD).
Opus 22, *Visions fugitives:*
#3-6, 8, 9, 11, 14, 15, 18, performed by S. Richter.
Memr 991002 (CD).
Opus 22, *Visions fugitives:*
#3, 6, 9, performed by S. Richter.
DG 2543 812 (LP), 1982; DG 423573-2 GDO (CD).
Opus 22, *Visions fugitives:*
#3, 10, 11, & 16, performed by D. Bashkirov.
Melodiya D 04860/1 (LP).
Opus 22, *Visions fugitives:*
#3, 11, performed by D. Bashkirov.
Melodiya D 0005156/7 (LP).
Opus 22, *Visions fugitives:*
#10, 11, 16, & 17, performed by E. Kissin.
Melodiya SUCD 10-00094 (CD).
RCA 60051-2-RC (CD), RCA 60051-4-RC (Cassette).
Opus 22, *Visions fugitives:*
#10, 15, 17, 18, performed by J. Sanromà.
HMV EC 115, Victor 1623, 1940.

Opus 28, *Sonata #3,* performed by G. Axelrod.
  Melodiya D 16943/4 (LP).
Opus 28, *Sonata #3,* performed by A. Bernheim. Vega C 35, A 229.
Opus 28, *Sonata #3,* performed by M. Béroff. EMI 2C 06973000.
Opus 28, *Sonata #3,* performed by S. Cherkassy.
  Am. Vox set 624, 1948.
Opus 28, *Sonata #3,* performed by A. Cigoli.
  Nuova Era 6718-DM (CD).
Opus 28, *Sonata #3,* performed by S. Contreras. CM 17.
Opus 28, *Sonata #3,* performed by R. Cornman.
  Decca LXT 2836, FST 153120; London LL 748 (LP).
Opus 28, *Sonata #3,* performed by B. Davidovich.
  Phil 412 742-1PH, Phil 412 742-2PH (CD).
Opus 28, *Sonata #3,* performed by E. Gilels. MACD 746 (CD).
Opus 28, *Sonata #3,* performed by G. Graffman.
  Columbia 5844 (LP), 1963;
  CBS MYK-37806 (CD), CBS MYT-37806 (Cassette);
  CBS CD 44876 (CD), CBS 40-44876 (Cassette).
Opus 28, *Sonata #3,* performed by C. Horsley. HMV C3941.
Opus 28, *Sonata #3,* performed by Jenkins.
  Kingsmill Gaudeamus KRS 37 (LP).
Opus 28, *Sonata #3,* performed by V. Kamenikova.
  Supraphon 1111 3374.
Opus 28, *Sonata #3,* performed by N. Magaloff.
  Disques Montaigne MAG 8941 (CD).
Opus 28, *Sonata #3,* performed by McIntyre. Artist 00291.
Opus 28, *Sonata #3,* performed by L. Pennario.
  Capitol P8376 (LP), 1957.
Opus 28, *Sonata #3,* performed by D. Pescatori. AS 5010 (CD).
Opus 28, *Sonata #3,* performed by Pollack. MK 1513.
Opus 28, *Sonata #3,* performed by R. Sadowsky. Prize, set A1.
Opus 28, *Sonata #3,* performed by S. Scheja. Bis 155 (LP).
Opus 28, *Sonata #3,* performed by Seow. Columbia MS-6925.
Opus 28, *Sonata #3,* performed by J. Shin' Ar.
  Pick. MCD 67 (CD), 1991.
Opus 28, *Sonata #3,* performed by G. Tacchino.
  Pierre Verany PV 791022 (CD), 1990.
Opus 28, *Sonata #3,* performed by T. Ury. Argo ATM 1006.
Opus 28, *Sonata #3,* performed by E. Varvarova.
  Chant du monde LDC 2781053 (LP).

Opus 28, *Sonata #3*, performed by S. Weissenberg.
Columbia ML 2099 (LP), 1950.

Opus 29, *Sonata #4*, performed by R. Cornman.
London LL 748 (LP).

Opus 29, *Sonata #4*, performed by A. de Raco.
Argo Odyssey LDC 520.

Opus 29, *Sonata #4*, performed by I. Gamulin.
MAVA MVA 1 (LP), 1984.

Opus 29, *Sonata #4*, performed by E. Malinin.
Angel 35402; Melodiya D 09387/8 (LP).

Opus 29, *Sonata #4*, performed by N. Petrov.
Melodiya SUCD 10-00207 (CD); Olympia OCD 280 (CD), 1991.

Opus 29, *Sonata #4*, performed by S. Richter.
Rococo 2143 (LP); Discocorp RR 467; AS Disc AS 334 (CD).

Opus 29, *Sonata #4*, performed by J. Zak.
Melodiya D 2802/3 (LP), D 029077/8 (LP).

Opus 31, *Tales of the Old Grandmother*, performed by M. Deyanova.
Nimbus NI-5176 (CD).

Opus 31, *Tales of the Old Grandmother*, performed by A. Foldes.
Vox PLP 6590.

Opus 31, *Tales of the Old Grandmother*, performed by
A. Goldenweiser. Melodiya 2576/7 (LP).

Opus 31, *Tales of the Old Grandmother*, performed by
C. Hugonnard-Roche.
Quantum QM 6913 (CD), QM 2008 (Cassette).

Opus 31, *Tales of the Old Grandmother*, performed by I. Janssen.
Globe GLO-5015 (CD), 1989.

Opus 31, *Tales of the Old Grandmother*, performed by
V. Kameníková. Supraphon 1111 3374.

Opus 31, *Tales of the Old Grandmother*, performed by V. Merzhanov.
MCA Classics/Melodiya MCD-32111 (CD),
MLC-32122 (Cassette), 1990.

Opus 31, *Tales of the Old Grandmother*, performed by C. Ortiz.
HOS 1364.

Opus 31, *Tales of the Old Grandmother*, performed by D. Pescatori.
AS 5010 (CD).

Opus 31, *Tales of the Old Grandmother*, performed by V. Sofronitsky.
Melodiya 9047/8 (LP), 016161 (LP).

Opus 31, *Tales of the Old Grandmother,* performed by E. Varvarova.
Chant du monde LDC 2781053 (CD).
Opus 31, *Tales of the Old Grandmother,* performed by Y. Yeresko.
Melodiya 022073/4 (LP), 01649/50 (LP).

Opus 32, *Four Pieces,* performed by A. Foldes. Vox PLP 6590.
Opus 32, *Four Pieces,* performed by E. Varvarova.
Chant du monde LDC 2781053 (CD).
Opus 32, *Four Pieces:*
#1, "Dance," performed by E. Kissin.
RCA 60051-2-RC (CD), 60051-4-RC (Cassette).
Melodiya SUCD 10-00094 (CD).
Opus 32, *Four Pieces:*
#1, "Dance" and #4, "Waltz," performed by S. Richter.
Memr 991002 (CD).
Opus 32, *Four Pieces:*
#3, "Gavotte," performed by A. Antoniades.
Polydor 47369, 1963.
Opus 32, *Four Pieces:*
#3, "Gavotte," performed by H. Roloff. PV 36072.
Opus 32, *Four Pieces:*
#3, "Gavotte," performed by M. Voskresensky.
Melodiya 5934/5, 035279/80.

Opus 33-ter, "March" and "Scherzo" from *Love for Three Oranges,*
performed by E. Gilels. USSR 14755, 1947.
Opus 33-ter, "March" and "Scherzo" from *Love for Three Oranges,*
performed by T. Joselson. Olympia OLY 453 (CD).
Opus 33-ter, "March" from *Love for Three Oranges,* performed by
A. Antoniades. Polydor 47369, 1939.
Opus 33-ter, "March" from *Love for Three Oranges,* performed by
L. Berman. Columbia M 34545 (LP), 1978.
Opus 33-ter, "March" from *Love for Three Oranges,* performed by
M. de Valmalete. Polydor 95175, 1928.
Opus 33-ter, "March" from *Love for Three Oranges,* performed by
B. Douglas. RCA 60779-2-RC (CD).
Opus 33-ter, "March" from *Love for Three Oranges,* performed by
P. Entremont. Columbia D3S-791 (LP).
Opus 33-ter, "March" from *Love for Three Oranges,* performed by
A. Foldes. Con. 5033 in set 22, 1947.

Opus 33-ter, "March" from *Love for Three Oranges,* performed by
E. Gilels. Chant du monde LDA 8104.
Opus 33-ter, "March" from *Love for Three Oranges,* performed by
T. Nikolaieva. Reli CR 911026 (CD), 1991.
Opus 33-ter, "March" from *Love for Three Oranges,* performed by
A. Rubinstein. Ermitage ERM 108S (CD).
Opus 33-ter, "March" from *Love for Three Oranges,* performed by
A. Rubinstein. ARL2-2359 (LP), ARK2-2359 (Cassette).
Opus 33-ter, "March" from Love for Three Oranges, performed by
G. Tacchino. Pierre Verany PV 791022 (CD), 1990.

Opus 38, *Sonata #5,* performed by A. Brendel.
Everest SBDR 3385 (LP), 1975.
Opus 38, *Sonata #5,* performed by R. Cornman. London LL 553.
Opus 38, *Sonata #5,* performed by H. Graf.
Period SPL 599 (LP); Cpt. MC 20075.
Opus 38, *Sonata #5,* performed by M. Grunberg.
Melodiya D 10333/4 (LP).
Opus 38, *Sonata #5,* performed by E. Novitskaya.
Melodiya/Angel S-40164.
Opus 38, *Sonata #5,* performed by J. Osorio.
Academy Sound and Vision DCA555 (LP), 1986;
CDDCA555 (CD), 1989; ZCDCA555 (Cassette).
Opus 38, *Sonata #5,* performed by P. Stepan. SUA ST 50697.
Opus 38, *Sonata #5,* performed by A. Vedernikov.
Melodiya D 6325/6 (LP), D 033635/6 (LP).

Opus 43b, *Divertimento,* performed by A. Verdernikov.
Melodiya 10013/4, 033635/6.

Opus 45, *Choses en soi,* performed by B. Bekhterev.
Melodiya 03155/6.
Opus 45A, "Chose en soi," performed by M. Yerdina.
Melodiya 03113/4.
Opus 45B, "Chose en soi," performed by V. Pleshakov.
Orion ORS 6915 (LP), 1969.

Opus 52, *Six Transcriptions,* performed by A. Ginsburg.
Melodiya D 019711/2 (LP).

Opus 52, *Six Transcriptions:*
#2, "Rondo" from *The Prodigal Son,* performed by S. Richter.
Memr 991002 (CD).

Opus 54, *Two Sonatinas,* performed by D. Rubinstein.
Musical Heritage Society MHS-1794.
Opus 54, *Two Sonatinas,* performed by M. Voskresensky.
Melodiya D 6325/6 (LP), D 035279/80 (LP).

Opus 59, *Three Pieces,* performed by G. Axelrod.
Melodiya D 16943/4 (LP).
Opus 59, *Three Pieces:*
#2, "Landscape" and #3, "Sonatina pastorale,"
performed by S. Richter. Memr 991002 (CD).
Opus 59, *Three Pieces:*
#3, "Sonatina pastorale," performed by R. Yassa.
Pavane ADW 7145 (LP), 1982; ADW 1799 (CD), 1990.

Opus 62, *Pensées,* performed by B. Bekhterev. Melodiya SM 03155/6.
Opus 62, *Pensées,* performed by A. Vedernikov.
Melodiya 10013/4 (LP), 033635/6 (LP).

Opus 65, *Music for Children,* performed by R. Bobitskaya.
Chant du monde LDC 288034 (CD); KA 488034 (Cassette).
Opus 65, *Music for Children,* performed by Gresko.
London STS-15470.
Opus 65, *Music for Children,* performed by R. Lev.
Concert Hall CHC-26; CHS Set AC, 1946.
Opus 65, *Music for Children,* performed by D. Pescatori.
AS 5010 (CD).
Opus 65, *Music for Children,* performed by M. Pressler.
MGM E3010 (LP).
Opus 65, *Music for Children,* performed by I. Zhukov.
Melodiya D 106885/6 (LP).
Opus 65, *Music for Children:*
#1-4, 6-8, 10-11, performed by M. Baslawskaya.
Globe GLO 5082 (CD), 1992.
Opus 65, *Music for Children:*
#6, "Waltz," performed by L. Rév.
Hyperion CDA66185 (CD), 1987; KA 66185 (Cassette), 1986.

Opus 75, *Ten Pieces from "Romeo and Juliet,"* performed by
  V. Ashkenazy. Decca SXL 3646, London 6573.
Opus 75, *Ten Pieces from "Romeo and Juliet,"* performed by
  L. Berman.
  DG 2531095 (LP); DG 3301095 (Cassette), 1979;
  DG 431170-2GGA (CD), DG 431170-4GGA (Cassette), 1991.
Opus 75, *Ten Pieces from "Romeo and Juliet,"* performed by
  S. de Groote. Finlandia 309; FACD 703 (CD), 1992.
Opus 75, *Ten Pieces from "Romeo and Juliet,"* performed by
  A. Gavrilov. EMI ASD 3802.
Opus 75, *Ten Pieces from "Romeo and Juliet,"* performed by
  C. Hugonnard-Roche.
  Quantum QM 6913 (CD), QM 2008 (Cassette).
Opus 75, *Ten Pieces from "Romeo and Juliet,"* performed by
  T. Joselson. Olympia OLY 453 (CD).
Opus 75, *Ten Pieces from "Romeo and Juliet,"* performed by
  A. Kubalek. Golden Crest 7057.
Opus 75, *Ten Pieces from "Romeo and Juliet,"* performed by
  H. Neuhaus. Monitor 2064.
Opus 75, *Ten Pieces from "Romeo and Juliet,"* performed by
  C. Ortiz. HQS 1393, 1977.
Opus 75, *Ten Pieces from "Romeo and Juliet,"* performed by
  G. Tacchino. Pierre Verany PV 791022 (CD), 1990.
Opus 75, *Ten Pieces from "Romeo and Juliet"* (selections),
  performed by A. Gavrilov. EMI ASD 3571/Angel S 37486.
Opus 75, *Ten Pieces from "Romeo and Juliet"*:
  #2, "Scene," performed by A. Gavrilov.
  SQ ASD 3571, TC ASD-3571, 1978.
Opus 75, *Ten Pieces from "Romeo and Juliet"*:
  #2, "Scene"; #4, "Young Juliet"; #6, "The Montagues and the
  Capulets"; #7, "Friar Laurence"; #8, "Mercutio"; #9, "Dance of
  the Girls with Lilies"; and #10, "Romeo Bids Juliet Farewell";
  performed by B. Davidovich.
  Phil 412 742-2PH (CD), 1987.
Opus 75, *Ten Pieces from "Romeo and Juliet"*:
  #2, "Scene"; #5, "Masks"; #6, "The Montagues and the
  Capulets"; #8, "Mercutio"; #9, "Dance of the Girls with Lilies";
  and #10, "Romeo Bids Juliet Farewell"; performed by A. Madzar.
  Nuov 6897 (CD), 1989.

Opus 75, *Ten Pieces from "Romeo and Juliet"*:
    #2, "Scene" and #9, "Dance of the Girls with Lilies,"
    performed by L. Berman. DG 2543 526, 3343 526, 1971.
Opus 75, *Ten Pieces from "Romeo and Juliet"*:
    #4, "Young Juliet"; #6, "The Montagues and the Capulets";
    and #10, "Romeo Bids Juliet Farewell"; performed by L. Lortie.
    Chandos CHAN-8733 (CD), ABTD-1373 (Cassette).
Opus 75, *Ten Pieces from "Romeo and Juliet"*:
    #10, "Romeo Bids Juliet Farewell," performed by V. Feltsman.
    CBS MK-44818 (CD), MT-44818 (Cassette).
Opus 75, *Ten Pieces from "Romeo and Juliet"*:
    #5, "Masks" and #10, "Romeo Bids Juliet Farewell,"
    performed by V. Ashkenazy. London CS-6573.
Opus 75, *Ten Pieces from "Romeo and Juliet"*:
    #10, "Romeo Bids Juliet Farewell," performed by A. Gavrilov.
    EMI EG 290326-1, EG 290326-4, 1985.

Opus 77-bis, "Gavotte" from *Hamlet,* performed by A. Vedernikov.
    Melodiya D 017091/2 (LP).

Opus 82, *Sonata #6,* performed by W. Akl.
    Thesis THC 28022 (CD), 1990.
Opus 82, *Sonata #6,* performed by D. Alexeyev.
    Melodiya SM 03599-600.
Opus 82, *Sonata #6,* performed by M. Béroff.
    EMI 2C 06973000 (LP).
Opus 82, *Sonata #6,* performed by J. Boyk.
    Performance Recordings PR8 (CD).
Opus 82, *Sonata #6,* performed by R. Cornman.
    Decca FST 513087; London LL 902.
Opus 82, *Sonata #6,* performed by W. Delony.
    Centaur CRC 2064 (CD), 1991.
Opus 82, *Sonata #6,* performed by P. Donohoe.
    EMI ASD 4321 (LP); TCC ASD 4321;
    Angel DS-38010 (CD), 1982; Angel CDC-54281 (CD);
    EMI CDC754281-2 (CD); EMI EL754381-4 (Cassette), 1991.
Opus 82, *Sonata #6,* performed by Friedman. Orion 79341.
Opus 82, *Sonata #6,* performed by S. Hough.
    Academy Sound and Vision AMM 157 (LP),
    ZC AMM 157 (Cassette), CD AMM 157 (CD), 1989.

Opus 82, *Sonata #6*, performed by T. Joselson.
Olympia OCD-350 (CD), 1990.
Opus 82, *Sonata #6*, performed by E. Kissin.
Sony SK 45931 (CD), ST 45931 (Cassette), 1990;
RCA 60443-2-RC (CD), 60443-4-RC (Cassette).
Opus 82, *Sonata #6*, performed by V. Krainev.
MCA Classics AED 68019 (CD), AEC 68019 (Cassette), 1990.
Opus 82, *Sonata #6*, performed by V. Merzhanov.
USSR 14100/2, 14105-9, 13745/6A, 1947.
Opus 82, *Sonata #6*, performed by K. W. Paik.
Dante PSG 9126 (CD).
Opus 82, *Sonata #6*, performed by J. Pálenícek.
U.G. 51239/41 (G 23046/8; Sup. 11502/4).
Opus 82, *Sonata #6*, performed by L. Pennario. Capitol P8113 (LP).
Opus 82, *Sonata #6*, performed by N. Petrov.
Melodiya SUCD 10-00207 (CD); Olympia OCD 280 (CD), 1991.
Opus 82, *Sonata #6*, performed by Pettaway. CRS 8526 (LP).
Opus 82, *Sonata #6*, performed by W. Plagge.
Simax PSC-1036 (CD), 1989.
Opus 82, *Sonata #6*, performed by I. Pogorelich.
DG 2532093; DG 413363-2 GH (CD), 1984.
Opus 82, *Sonata #6*, performed by S. Richter.
Ermitage ERM 113 (CD); Praga PR 250 015 (CD).
Opus 82, *Sonata #6*, performed by Rust. Protone PR-158 (LP).
Opus 82, *Sonata #6*, performed by S. Scheja. Bis 155 (LP).
Opus 82, *Sonata #6*, performed by R. Silverman.
Orion ORS 78328 (LP), 1979.
Opus 82, *Sonata #6*, performed by A. Slobodyanik.
Melodiya/Angel S-40109.
Opus 82, *Sonata #6*, performed by E. Soifertis-Lukjanenko.
Partridge 1127-2 (CD).
Opus 82, *Sonata #6*, performed by Van Cliburn.
RCA 7941-2-RG (CD), 7941-4-RG (Cassette);
RCA GD87941 (CD), GK87941 (Cassette).
Opus 82, *Sonata #6*, performed by E. Varvarova.
Chant du monde LDC 2781053 (CD).

Opus 83, *Sonata #7*, performed by W. Akl. Thesis THC 82022 (CD).
Opus 83, *Sonata #7*, performed by V. Ashkenazy.
Decca SXL 6346, London 6573, (1968).

Opus 83, *Sonata #7,* Opus 83, performed by M. Béroff.
EMI 2C 06973000.
Opus 83, *Sonata #7,* performed by Y. Bronfman.
CBS MK-44680 (CD), MT-44680 (Cassette), 1989.
Opus 83, *Sonata #7,* performed by L. Cabasso. Valois V 4655 (CD).
Opus 83, *Sonata #7,* performed by R. Cornman.
Decca FST 153087, London LL902 (LP).
Opus 83, *Sonata #7,* performed by A. di Bonaventura.
Sine ULDD-13.
Opus 83, *Sonata #7,* performed by P. Donohoe.
Angel CDC-54281 (CD); EMI EL754381-4 (Cassette), 1991.
Opus 83, *Sonata #7,* performed by B. Douglas.
RCA 60779-2-RC (CD).
Opus 83, *Sonata #7,* performed by E. Gilels. Bruno 14049.
Opus 83, *Sonata #7,* performed by Glenn Gould.
Columbia MS 7173 (LP), 1969; CBS M3K-42150 (CD);
Nuova Era 2273 (CD), 1989; Memories HR 4415-16 (CD).
Opus 83, *Sonata #7,* performed by F. Gulda. Decca AK 1992-4, 1948.
Opus 83, *Sonata #7,* performed by Hollander. Angel S-36025.
Opus 83, *Sonata #7,* performed by V. Horowitz.
Victor 11-9100/1; Victor Set M 1042, 1946;
RCA Victor LM 1016; RCA Victor LD 7021;
RCA 60377-2-RG (CD), 60377-4-RG (Cassette).
Opus 83, *Sonata #7,* performed by S. Igolinsky. DG 2538 378.
Opus 83, *Sonata #7,* performed by T. Joselson.
RCA ARL1-2753 (LP), ARK1-2753 (Cassette).
Opus 83, *Sonata #7,* performed by V. Kamyshov.
Melodiya D 024249/50 (LP).
Opus 83, *Sonata #7,* performed by M. Kodama. ASV DCA786 (CD).
Opus 83, *Sonata #7,* performed by V. Krainev.
MCA Classics AED 68019 (CD), AEC 68019 (Cassette), 1990.
Opus 83, *Sonata #7,* performed by G. Landes.
Stradivari Classics SCD-6069 (CD), 1990;
SMC-6069 (Cassette), 1990.
Opus 83, *Sonata #7,* performed by Y. Mogilevsky. MK 418021 (CD).
Opus 83, *Sonata #7,* performed by I. Nadas. Dover HCR 5215 (LP).
Opus 83, *Sonata #7,* performed by K.W. Paik. Dante PSG 9126 (CD).
Opus 83, *Sonata #7,* performed by M. Pletnev. ASD 3715, 1979.
Opus 83, *Sonata #7,* performed by Pollack. MK 1513.

Opus 83, *Sonata #7*, performed by M. Pollini.
DG 5230 225 (LP), 1972; DG 2740 229 (LP), 1982;
DG 419202-2 GH (CD), 1986.
Opus 83, *Sonata #7*, performed by R. Press.
Meridian CDE 84160 (CD),
Meridian KE77 160 (Cassette), 1990.
Opus 83, *Sonata #7*, performed by S. Richter.
Chant du monde LDX 78358 (LP), LDXP 8249;
Wergo WER 60004 (LP), WER 6221-24 (CD);
Turnabout 34359; Artia 154.
Opus 83, *Sonata #7*, performed by P. Rutman.
Odyssey Y 34634 (LP), 1978.
Opus 83, *Sonata #7*, performed by A. Slobodyanik.
AED 10107 (CD).
Opus 83, *Sonata #7*, performed by B. Snyder.
Golden Crest RE 7058 (LP).
Opus 83, *Sonata #7*, performed by G. Sokolov.
Melodiya D 026491/2 (LP).
Opus 83, *Sonata #7*, performed by A. Toradze.
Angel CDC-47607 (CD), 4DS-37360 (Cassette).
Opus 83, *Sonata #7* (third movement), performed by M. Argerich.
Hunt Productions HUNTCD 574 (CD); Arkadia 574 (CD).
Opus 83, *Sonata #7* (third movement), performed by V. Horowitz.
RCA Victor LM 6014.

Opus 84, *Sonata #8*, performed by W. Akl.
Thesis THC 82023 (CD), 1990.
Opus 84, *Sonata #8*, performed by V. Ashkenazy.
Decca SXL 6346/London 6573 (LP), 1968.
Opus 84, *Sonata #8*, performed by D. Bashkirov.
Melodiya S 01651/2, D 021041/2 (LP).
Opus 84, *Sonata #8*, performed by L. Berman.
HUN HLX-90048-1 (LP); DG 2530 678 (LP), 1976.
Opus 84, *Sonata #8*, performed by Y. Bronfman.
CBS MK-44680 (CD), MT-44680 (Cassette), 1989.
Opus 84, *Sonata #8*, performed by R. Cornman. London 748 (LP).
Opus 84, *Sonata #8*, performed by Y. Egorov.
Channel Classics CG 9215 (CD).
Opus 84, *Sonata #8*, performed by S. de Groote.
Finlandia 309; FACD 703 (CD), 1992.

Opus 84, *Sonata #8,* performed by A. di Bonaventura.
Classic Editions CE 1032 (LP).

Opus 84, *Sonata #8,* performed by P. Donohoe.
Angel CDC-54281 (CD); EMI EL754381-4 (Cassette), 1991.

Opus 84, *Sonata #8,* performed by A. Gavrilov. EMI ASD 3802 (LP).

Opus 84, *Sonata #8,* performed by E. Gilels.
Eurodisc 86 323 (LP); Columbia/Melodiya M-33824.

Opus 84, *Sonata #8,* performed by T. Joselson. RCA ARL1-1570.

Opus 84, *Sonata #8,* performed by V. Krainev. Melodiya SM 03721/2.

Opus 84, *Sonata #8,* performed by F. Moyer.
GM Recordings 2011 (LP), 2011T (Cassette).

Opus 84, *Sonata #8,* performed by T. Nikolayeva.
Melodiya D 015077/8 (LP).

Opus 84, *Sonata #8,* performed by N. Petrov.
Melodiya SUCD 10-00200 (CD).

Opus 84, *Sonata #8,* performed by N. Posnjakow.
MTM 0500CD (CD), 1990.

Opus 84, *Sonata #8,* performed by S. Richter.
DG 423573-2 GDO (CD), 1988; DG SPLM 138766 (LP), 1962;
DG 2543812 (LP), 1980; DG 2538073 (LP); Rococo 2143 (LP);
Pyramid PYR 13503 (CD).

Opus 95, *Three Pieces From "Cinderella":*
#2, "Gavotte," performed by S. Richter. Memr 991001 (CD).

Opus 96, *Three Pieces From "War and Peace" and "Lermontov,"*
performed by Drake. Orion 688 (LP).

Opus 96, *Three Pieces from "War and Peace" and "Lermontov,"*
performed by L. Mayorga. Sheffield Lab SLS-505 (CD).

Opus 96, *Three Pieces from "War and Peace" and "Lermontov":*
#1, "Waltz" from *War and Peace,* performed by B. Douglas.
Orion 688 (LP).

Opus 96, *Three Pieces from "War and Peace" and "Lermontov":*
#1, "Waltz" from *War and Peace,* performed by S. Richter.
Memr 991002 (CD).

Opus 97, *Ten Pieces from "Cinderella,"* performed by T. Joselson.
Olympia OLY 453 (CD).

Opus 97, *Ten Pieces from "Cinderella,"* performed by M. Pressler.
MGM 3192.

Opus 97, *Ten Pieces from "Cinderella,"* performed by R. Yassa.
Pavane ADW 7145 (LP), 1982; ADW 7199 (CD), 1990.
Opus 97, *Ten Pieces from "Cinderella"* (selections), performed by
C. Ortiz. HQS 1393, 1977.
Opus 97, *Ten Pieces from "Cinderella"*:
#3, "Autumn Fairy" and #6, "Orientale,"
performed by S. Richter. Memr 991001 (CD).
Opus 97, *Ten Pieces from "Cinderella"*:
#10, "Adagio," performed by B. Douglas.
RCA 60779-2-RC (CD), 1992.

Opus 102, *Six Pieces from "Cinderella"*:
#1, "Waltz" and #3, "Quarrel," performed by S. Richter.
Memr 991001 (CD).
Opus 102, *Six Pieces from "Cinderella"*:
#4, "Waltz" and #6, "Amoroso," performed by B. Douglas.
RCA RD 60779 (CD), 1992.

Opus 103, *Sonata #9,* performed by W. Akl.
Thesis THC 82023 (CD), 1990.
Opus 103, *Sonata #9,* performed by C. Hugonnard-Roche.
Quantum QM 6913 (CD), QM 2008 (Cassette).
Opus 103, *Sonata #9,* performed by T. Joselson.
RCA ARL1-2753 (LP), ARK1-2753 (Cassette).
Opus 103, *Sonata #9,* performed by J. Kalichstein.
Vanguard VC S10048 (LP), 1969.
Opus 103, *Sonata #9,* performed by Margulis.
Christophorus CD-74563.
Opus 103, *Sonata #9,* performed by S. Perticarolli.
Ermitage ERM 402 (CD).
Opus 103, *Sonata #9,* performed by N. Petrov.
Melodiya SUCD 10-00200 (CD).
Opus 103, *Sonata #9,* performed by M. Pressler. MGM 3192.
Opus 103, *Sonata #9,* performed by S. Richter.
Chant du monde LDXP 8249; Chant du monde LDX 78538 (LP);
Wergo WER 60004 (LP); Monitor MC-2034 (LP);
Praga PR 250 015 (CD); Memr 991001 (CD).
Opus 103, *Sonata #9,* performed by G. Sokolov.
Opus 111 OPS 40-9104 (CD).

Opus 135, *Sonata #5* (revised version), performed by E. Novitskaya. Melodiya-Angel. SR 40164.

Waltzes (Schubert-Prokofiev), performed by F. Chiu. Harmonia Mundi HMU 907054 (CD), HMU 497954 (Cassette).

Waltzes (Schubert-Prokofiev), performed by V. Leyetchkiss. Orion ORS 80378 (LP), 1980.

INDEX

INDEX OF PROKOFIEV'S WORKS

Published Piano Works of Prokofiev

Opus 1, *Sonata #1*, F minor, 1, 9, 22, 27, 32, 33, 48, 49-50

Opus 2, *Four Etudes*, 9, 17, 21, 24, 32, 33, 36, 39, 40, 43, 52, 132-134

Opus 3, *Four Pieces* ("Story," "Jest," "March," "Phantom"), 9, 13-14, 16, 20, 22, 24, 25, 28, 32, 39, 43, 45, 48, 49, 55, 101-103

Opus 4, *Four Pieces* ("Reminiscence," "Elan," "Despair," "Diabolical Suggestion"), 4, 9, 17, 20, 21, 23, 24, 26, 28, 32, 33, 42, 49, 53, 55, 101, 104-106, 135

Opus 11, *Toccata,* 3, 4, 8, 9, 17, 22, 25, 29, 33, 34, 35, 37, 44, 46, 53, 132, 137

Opus 12, *Ten Pieces* "March," "Gavotte," "Rigaudon," "Mazurka," "Capriccio," "Legend," "Prelude," "Allemande," "Humoresque Scherzo," "Scherzo"), 9, 15-16, 19, 20, 23, 24, 28, 33, 37, 52, 53, 101, 106-111

Opus 14, *Sonata #2*, D minor, 2, 4, 9, 17, 18, 20, 25, 26, 28, 29-30, 31, 32, 37, 38, 39, 40, 43, 45, 46, 47, 48, 49, 50, 51, 52, 90, 142-144

Opus 17, *Sarcasms,* 9, 25, 41-42, 44, 132, 134-137

Opus 22, *Visions fugitives,* 3, 9, 31, 40, 47, 101, 112-122, 123

Opus 28, *Sonata #3*, A minor, 8, 9, 50, 145, 149

Opus 29, *Sonata #4,* C minor, 8, 9, 45, 50, 145-147

Opus 31, *Tales of the Old Grandmother,* 55, 101, 123-125

Opus 32, *Four Pieces* ("Dance," "Minuet," "Gavotte," "Waltz"), 55, 101, 125-127

Opus 38, *Sonata #5* (revised as Opus 135), 55, 56, 57, 60, 64, 67, 68, 69, 147-149

Opus 45, *Choses en soi,* 55, 56, 58, 59, 61, 65, 69, 71, 132, 137-139

Opus 54, *Two Sonatinas,* 55, 57, 58, 60, 64, 101, 128-129, 158

Opus 59, *Three Pieces* ("Landscape," "Promenade," "Sonatina pastorale"), 55, 65, 69, 71, 101, 130-131

Unpublished and unfinished works

ABOUT THE AUTHOR

Dr. Stephen Fiess, a native of Stratford, Ontario, Canada, holds an Associateship Diploma from the Royal Conservatory of Music of Toronto and a Bachelor of Music degree in Piano Performance from the University of Western Ontario. He received his Master of Music degree in Piano Performance from Indiana University, where he was a student of the late British concert pianist John Ogdon. In 1989, he received his Doctor of Musical Arts Degree in Piano Performance, Literature, and Pedagogy from the University of Colorado at Boulder. He also holds an Associateship Certificate from the American Guild of Organists.

Dr. Fiess was a prizewinner in the Krenek Division of the 1989 Joanna Hodges International Piano Competition. He has also composed ballets that have been performed in Colorado and at the International Dance Festival of Havana, Cuba.

His interest in Prokofiev's piano music led to a doctoral dissertation on that subject. Dr. Fiess has also presented several lecture-recitals in honor of the Prokofiev Centennial in 1991 and performed selections from Prokofiev's *Visions fugitives* at the 1991 National Convention of the College Music Society.